TRANS~~~~~~~~~G
your pet ~~~~~~r

LEARN WHAT THEIR BEHAVIOR
SAYS ABOUT YOU TO TRAIN
SMARTER, NOT HARDER

BY DENISE MANGE

TRANSLATING YOUR PET'S BEHAVIOR
Copyright © 2024 by Denise Mange

All rights reserved. No part of this publication may be reproduced, distributed, or transmitted in any form or by any means without the prior written permission of the author, except in the case of brief quotations used in book reviews and critical articles.

All service marks, product names, and trademarks belong to their respective owners.

Although every effort has been made to ensure the information in this book was correct and best practice at press time, the author and publisher do not assume and hereby disclaim any liability to any party for any loss, damage, or disruption caused by errors or omissions, whether such errors or omissions result from negligence, accident, or any other cause. Especially with aggression or anxiety, please consult a qualified professional.

Materials, techniques, and information shared in this book are provided for informational purposes only and must not be construed as personal medical advice. Before making any changes, participants should consult their healthcare providers or seek medical or veterinary advice.

Although the examples in this book reflect real-life situations, they are not necessarily descriptions of actual people but, in some cases, are composites created from many years of working with countless pet guardians in many varied contexts.

ISBN 979-8-9901494-0-3

Printed in the United States of America by Pet Prana® LLC

Dedicated to our animal companions.

To my soul pack of pet parents who have shared so openly, thank you for contributing to this work.

Preface
Train Smarter, Not Harder

"**D**ogs are man's best friend." We've all heard it and immediately think – *yes*! But what if their role goes deeper than that? What are those soulful eyes, mischievous stunts, and bouts of barking trying to tell us? And how about other pets: cats, birds, hamsters, and even snakes?

These were the kinds of questions I asked myself as a kid. I'd wonder: *If our pets could talk, what would they say? Why do the three caterpillars who are supposed to sting like fire peacefully crawl into my palm, then retreat to their leaf-strewn aquarium on my nightstand?*

I spent a lot of time observing my childhood animal companions—fish, turtles, a baby chicken, a mouse. By age 7, I became a vegetarian. I understood that our energy is tied to the energy and behavior of animals. This realization would become my life's passion.

But then, life happens. Enter adult responsibility and serious new mindsets. University beckons, careers need building, financial survival becomes pressing, and time management robs us of our pet projects and passions.

But in 2012, everything changed. Post-graduation and post-Madison Avenue, I had my *a-ha* moment. I left my corporate job in advertising and began working as a traditional dog trainer. About a year in, I knew there had to be more that could be done to honor the relationship between humans and their pets beyond simply teaching them how to sit and fetch.

That's when I began combining traditional dog training with animal communication and pet numerology. After working with hundreds of clients over the span of ten years, I developed a roadmap of how our pets' behavior speaks to our broader mindsets, patterns, habits, and attitudes and acts as a reflection of self.

This is so important because when we understand the energetic and emotional motivation driving our pet's behavior, we can identify how that same energetic pattern may be manifesting itself more broadly in our friendships, romantic relationships, family life, and career. Once we understand the motivation, we can change our mindset around it and create new outcomes for ourselves and our furry companions.

Perhaps you're interested in pet training because—although you love your dog—you can identify with feeling frustrated by their behavior. Maybe you find yourself losing patience when your furry friend doesn't seem to be listening. Or maybe your pet is acting out during walks, struggling with separation anxiety, or demanding attention when you're hoping for downtime.

Regardless, you're reading this book because you are looking to shift a dynamic between you and your pet. You are not alone. I've helped countless pet parents who felt the same way.

Together, we'll be digging into a completely new approach to pet guardianship that allows you, as a pet parent, to communicate and bond on deeper levels with your pet.

By the end of this book, you'll have learned a practical framework to translate what your pet is telling you through their behavior and a plan for addressing your pet's behavior mindfully through both traditional training techniques and energetic considerations. This combination will help you train smarter, not harder.

Whether you have tried implementing training but haven't seen results, you're interested in how your pet mirrors back bigger motivations, mindsets, habits, and views in your life more broadly, or you are simply interested in learning more about how our pets bring balance to our lives, energy, and surroundings, I hope this book helps you take a more mindful approach to pet guardianship.

Some of what is shared may resonate deeply with you, while some may not. Remember that although I am a pet expert, you are the authority for you and your pet, so I invite you to adopt as much of this material that is helpful and set aside any that is not. Thank you for being a part of this new vanguard in pet guardianship and part of a discussion on connecting more mindfully with our animal companions.

Nah Mutt Stay!

How to Use This Book

Whether you are looking for a mindful approach to dog training, how to translate your pet's behavior, or both, this book becomes your point of reference.

Although our philosophy applies to all animal companions, this content focuses on dogs. You can pick and choose how deeply you want to engage with the information, whether reading this book from cover to cover or focusing on specific chapters most pertinent to you and your pet.

As a resource that supports you and your furry friend from puppyhood to senior years, we invite you to return to its pages as new training opportunities arise in different phases of your life together.

The content is divided into two parts: **PART 1:** *Foundational Theories* and **PART 2:** *Practical Applications*.

What We'll Dig Into

- A new, groundbreaking philosophy in pet training that builds upon Abraham Maslow's widely accepted theory of motivation outlined in his Hierarchy of Needs and our Chakra System.
- A mindful approach to dog training proven to deliver transformative results.

- Easy-to-use references as you analyze your dog's behavior.
- Hands-on applications, including training basics, tools, and recommended supplies.
- Practical case studies.
- Training activities and mindful journaling prompts to better translate themes of each pet behavior to other areas in your life and see in hindsight how your mindsets and habits have shifted.

TABLE OF CONTENTS

PREFACE: TRAIN SMARTER, NOT HARDER I
HOW TO USE THIS BOOK IV

PART 1 : FOUNDATIONAL THEORIES *1*

A MINDFUL APPROACH TO DOG TRAINING 3
PETS AS MIRRORS & OUR INTERCONNECTEDNESS 5
HOW BELIEFS SHAPE OUR MINDSET 11
TRIGGERS & MINDSETS TO SHIFT 16
DIGGING INTO MOTIVATION WITH MASLOW'S PYRAMID 23
ENERGETIC OVERLAY: THE CHAKRA SYSTEM 30
OUR PROPRIETARY PROCESS TRANSLATING BEYOND BEHAVIOR[SM] 36
PRINCIPLES OF POSITIVE REINFORCEMENT TRAINING 42
READY? LET'S DIG IN. 50

PART 2 : PRACTICAL APPLICATIONS *53*

ON-LEASH REACTIVITY & BUILDING A FOUNDATION FOR SUCCESS 55
    TRANSLATING YOUR PET'S BEHAVIOR 63
    ON-LEASH REACTIVITY TRAINING 67
    ACTIVITIES 75
SEPARATION ANXIETY & CREATING LOVING BOUNDARIES 77
    TRANSLATING YOUR PET'S BEHAVIOR 84
    SEPARATION ANXIETY TRAINING 89
    ACTIVITIES 98

BARKING, NIPPING, JUMPING & STEPPING INTO YOUR POWER 105
   TRANSLATING YOUR PET'S BEHAVIOR 112
   MANAGING UNWANTED BEHAVIORS TRAINING 115
   ACTIVITIES 124

GUEST REACTIVITY & PUTTING YOURSELF FIRST 127
   TRANSLATING YOUR PET'S BEHAVIOR 134
   GUEST DESENSITIZATION TRAINING 138
   ACTIVITIES 148

BENEVOLENT LEADERSHIP & SPEAKING YOUR TRUTH 151
   TRANSLATING YOUR PET'S BEHAVIOR 158
   BENEVOLENT LEADERSHIP TRAINING 162
   ACTIVITIES 170

HOUSEBREAKING, ACCIDENTS & LEADING AN INTENTIONAL LIFE 173
   TRANSLATING YOUR PET'S BEHAVIOR 180
   HOUSEBREAKING TRAINING 183
   ACTIVITIES 191

MOMENTS OF CRISIS & UNDERSTANDING THE BIG PICTURE 195
   TRANSLATING YOUR PET'S BEHAVIOR 202
   PRACTICAL CONSIDERATIONS 206
   ACTIVITIES 216

IN SUMMATION: NAHMUTTSTAY® 221
   BONUS MATERIALS 224
   ABOUT THE AUTHOR 225
   DIG INTO ONLINE COURSES 226

Part 1: Foundational Theories

A Mindful Approach to Dog Training

So, what does it mean to train smarter, not harder? Many pet parents keep pushing the same training routine, spending hours practicing commands and trying the same techniques over and over. They are hoping to shift their animal companion's actions and responses but are not addressing a key component: the energetic dynamic motivating the behavior.

In these scenarios, a shift in mindset is crucial. Unless we approach our pet's behavior through a comprehensive lens, we won't see the results we want despite hours of training.

When we combine traditional training with the energetic factors—and effectively translate our pet's behavior in the process—we go from feeling frustrated, disregarded, and unheard to opening lines of communication that create meaningful change for ourselves and our pets.

Taking a mindful approach to training and connecting with our dogs will make all the difference. It allows us to train more effectively while seeing greater shifts and results.

However, this notion of combining traditional training with the energetic aspects of pet guardianship is new. Most pet training resources still view our animal companions' behavior as separate from ours. They recommend cookie-cutter methods that don't address the energy at the core of our pets' behavior. On the other end of the spectrum are conceptual, exoteric resources on the energetic roles pets play in our lives, but lack practical guidance. No one has brought the two together until now.

I am excited to offer the first philosophy to combine traditional dog training techniques with the energetic considerations of pet guardianship in a tangible and practical way, rooted in shared motivation and the seven major chakras.

I like to refer to this approach as *self-help for pet's sake* because when we connect mindfully with our animal companions, we vibe higher, and so do our pets. And when we are leading more empowered and fulfilling lives, our pets' behavior reflects it.

Through exploring the relationship with our pets as we teach them new behaviors, we embark on a deeper understanding of ourselves. And as we become more empowered, learn to set healthy boundaries, and find our authentic leadership style, our pets' behavior reflects it and our bond with them grows. As pet parents leveraging traditional training with energetic considerations of pet guardianship, we can train smarter, not harder.

Pets as Mirrors
& Our Interconnectedness

Our pets have always intended to connect with us on a deeper level. But only now are we, as pet parents, realizing their influence goes far beyond love and companionship. Great entertainers, confidants, healers, and teachers, they are inextricably linked to our well-being. Yet one of the most profound roles our animal companions take on is that of a mirror, reflecting back to us our own energetic terrain.

This interplay between humans and pets is a testament to our connection and the power animal companions hold to transform our lives.

When our animal companions are displaying behaviors like barking for attention, having accidents, or separation anxiety, it is important to understand that these behaviors serve as reflections of our innermost emotions and mindsets. They are likely drawing attention to broader habits, perceptions, or attitudes affecting our lives that need to be addressed.

For example, when a dog incessantly barks for attention, he may be mirroring our own desires for recognition, validation, or to feel heard in our career. If a cat exhibits skittishness or aggression, she may be echoing our own unresolved fears or anxieties in an intimate relationship. In this way, our animal companions highlight aspects of ourselves that we may not otherwise readily acknowledge.

Our pets also have a remarkable ability to tune into our energy, which can greatly influence their behavior. For example, a dog may be relaxed or playful if we are calm and content. When we are stressed out or anxious, he or she may mirror the same energy through restlessness, paw licking, or other signs of anxiety.

But how can you translate exactly what is being reflected when your dog is barking, your cat is having accidents, or your bird is pulling out their feathers?

Our pets' behavior is a catalyst to illicit feelings, sensations, thoughts, and memories. When observed mindfully, these provide insight into what our pets are communicating to us, including what beliefs, behaviors, mindsets, or habits in our lives need to be revisited, reaffirmed, or changed.

Let's put that philosophy to the test:

Take three deep breaths.

Think of a behavior your pet may be presenting. It could be barking, having accidents, or maybe even something you enjoy, like waking you in the morning with licks.

What emotions come up for you when you connect into this experience?

Where else in your life do you experience similar emotions? Does it trigger memories, past experiences, or remind you of another situation in your life?

What belief, behavior, mindset, or habit is at the core of that emotion, experience, or situation, and is it influencing other areas of your life?

If this belief, mindset or habit is unproductive or not creating desirable experiences, are you ready to make a change? If so, what's a new mindset or behavior that could lead to a better outcome?

Hang in there for a moment.

What insights did you take away?

Whether or not this exercise guided you to experience any sensations, memories, or even a-ha moments, know that as we progress through the chapters of this book, you'll gain tools and insight to revisit this exercise and pinpoint accurately and intuitively what your pet is trying to tell you through their behavior and your shared experiences.

Mirroring through Physical Issues

Our connection to pets extends beyond emotions. Animal companions can develop physical conditions that reflect their pet parents' own unaddressed physical or emotional issues, or as a response to dynamics within the home or pack.

Colonel, a pug living in New York City, is a great example of this. Like many city dogs, Colonel had a tendency to bark and lunge at passing dogs on walks. Despite demanding careers and the stress of planning a wedding abroad, Colonel's pet parents were committed to dedicating the necessary time to help him overcome this issue.

For weeks, they diligently documented their walks with Colonel in a shared journal, noting new triggers and strategies that seemed to work better than others in redirecting him on-leash.

They regularly reviewed these records, and in doing so, Colonel's parents realized that his on-leash reactions were worse on days they had arguments or stressful wedding planning meetings. Beyond that, they noticed that a recurring rash on Colonel's belly also coincided with these moments of tension in their relationship.

With this insight, they decided to work not only on Colonel's training but also on their own relationship. Just as his pet parents had committed to setting time aside to address Colonel's behavior, they did the same each night to calmly and compassionately address any lingering emotions, disagreements, misunderstandings, or unsettled feelings between them from the day.

The positive shifts were palpable. Both Colonel's on-leash reactivity and his belly rash became less frequent. And with the awareness of how their relationship influenced Colonel, any signs of him reverting to his old ways or the rash reappearing became an impetus for his pet parents to mindfully observe and address any unresolved tension or stressors. They adopted an effective and comprehensive approach to Colonel's behavior while staying consistent with traditional training methods and even extended these principles to behavioral challenges they were experiencing with their cat.

Colonel and his family learned what affects one member reverberates through all in the pack. They harnessed this understanding of the deep interconnectedness with our pets and paired it with consistent traditional training techniques to help them train smarter, not harder. For us to do the same, below are some important principles that help us use this realization to our advantage:

Be the Energy You Want to See. When working with pets, it's crucial to remember that your energy, voice, breath, and body language set the tone for your animal companion. Your demeanor and mindset communicate volumes to them. Exuding calm and grounded energy is one of the most effective ways to soothe your pet. A single grounding breath can transform the outcome of a walk or a training session.

Putting a Stop to Empathic Cycling. Pets absorb our energy, but as empathic pet parents, it is often a two-way street. If your pet reacts anxiously to certain situations, you might unconsciously absorb and reflect that anxiety. This creates a feedback loop, where your pet's anxiety triggers yours, and vice versa. Recognizing when, where, and how this energy exchange occurs can empower you to stop these cycles and create a more harmonious experience for both you and your pet.

Tailored Companionship

A pet's behavior and personality do not always directly reflect their humans' energy. They can also compensate for it. For example, in homes with heightened stress, overscheduling, and frenetic energy, animal companions might mirror these imbalances by becoming anxious and high-strung themselves. On the other hand, some pets act as natural balancers, compensating for the discordant energy in their environment. By exuding calm, stability, and groundedness, they effectively counterbalance their homes' energy and provide respite for family members.

Along those lines, pets often play different roles for pack members within a family. They can mirror and adapt their behaviors based on the energy and needs of the specific family member they are interacting with. For example, a dog might be perfectly well-behaved on a leash for one pet parent but exhibit reactivity with another.

Just as pet training is not a one-size-fits-all endeavor, our pet's response to their environment and the energetic role in our lives isn't either. Through their adaptability and capacity to connect deeply, our pets provide tailored companionship to best support each member of the pack.

Activity

ENERGY TRACKER CHART

Take a couple of days or an upcoming weekend to chart out how your energy has potentially influenced your dog's behavior and attitudes. Observe how your furry friend best responds to you. Journal your day alongside your dog's behavior, being mindful of cosmic activity, like full or new moons, stressors, or any shifts in your own energy that your pup may be reflecting back to you.

How Beliefs Shape Our Mindset

Our pets—and even animal guides—can help us lighten our energy in both literal and intangible ways. Through their behavior, they help us revisit old stories, beliefs, habits, patterns—and even belongings—to decide whether to keep them in our metaphoric library or release them to make room for new mindsets, possibilities, and outcomes.

During the winter of 2019, a powerful transformation began to unfold, orchestrated by my animal guides. Their presence became increasingly noticeable around my bookshelf, where I kept a collection of books that had journeyed with me since my high school days in Brazil. Their persistent appearances—along with a binge-watching session of a home decluttering series on Netflix—prompted an evaluation of all items on the bookshelf.

It was during one of these evaluations that the pivotal moment occurred. One book in particular caught my eye as I audited the bookshelf: Hemingway's *The Sun Also Rises*. I love Hemingway's writing and re-read that book often. As I leafed through the pages, I felt the gaze of my animal guides upon me, and intuitively, their message became clear: they wanted me to release and donate the book.

My stubbornness, however, led to a spirited debate in which I defended my reasons for holding on to it, culminating in a somewhat comical query to pose to animal guides: "Have you even read

Hemingway?" They responded with a resounding "No, but we've *felt* Hemingway."

As the layers of this dialogue continued to unfurl, I understood that, along with the book itself, they were encouraging me to release its essence—themes of longing, lack of connection, and unattainable happiness. Reluctantly, I agreed to let go of the book.

But the story did not end there, as my guides directed my attention back to the bookshelf where a sequence of titles was meticulously arranged. They included: Tim O'Brien's *The Things They Carried*, a book about the Trail of Tears called *And the Earth Shall Weep*, followed by a biography of Kurt Cobain called *Heavier than Heaven*, and last but not least, a biography of the band Pearl Jam called *Five Against One*.

The significance of these books became unmistakable. They embodied heavy vibrations I had physically and metaphorically carried across continents and throughout various phases of life. As a person who does not collect a lot of sentimental possessions, these books made up a significant part of my keepsakes and, as an extension, the energy of my home. My guides seemed to say, "It's time to let go."

In this exchange, a profound realization washed over me. It was necessary to let go of those books to make space for new energy. And so, I did.

By April, I understood the benefit of creating space. New energy made way for a profound and advanced understanding of ways our animal companions help us develop our intuition, expanding my work and relationship with animal companions.

This energetic exchange is representative of the role our pets play in helping us release outdated clutter, keepsakes, memories, habits, perceptions, and even beliefs that are limiting our personal growth. You may have experienced the same more tangibly with your dog lifting their leg on a souvenir or your cat clawing up an old dress.

Our pets teach us that unless we are willing to let go of the old, we can't create space for new energy, insights, habits, and outcomes to set in. And for humans, old energetic clutter often shows up in the form of limiting beliefs and mindsets. So, let's dig into what they are and how they shape our experiences, relationships, habits, and outcomes.

Beliefs That Limit Our Growth

Beliefs are stories we tell ourselves to quickly understand and process the world around us. Often rooted in our formative years, they serve as a means of survival, protection, or gaining acceptance. Our beliefs create a bias through which we perceive our experiences. If beneficial, they can propel us forward, and if limiting, they can hold us back.

Beliefs inform our mindsets, which shape our approach to life. Take, for example, the scenario of training your pet without seeing the changes you were expecting. As a result, a belief that your pet is choosing to ignore you begins to form. You believe that trying to affect change is hopeless because your pet never listens to you. And the consistency of this thought starts shaping the mindset through which you approach and experience training your pet. It becomes a self-fulfilling prophecy.

This preconception hinders your progress. And it's unlikely that this mindset is confined to training your pet; odds are, it also echoes in other areas of your life. This pattern of not feeling heard by your animal companion may trigger similar feelings or memories from your career or relationships. This belief that your pet deliberately ignores you during training mirrors a self-fulfilling belief that shapes the lens through which you perceive the world and judge interactions and dynamics in all areas of your life.

Yet, if you reassess this mindset, you may realize that your pet's behavior is not rooted in indifference but rather a result of impulse control challenges or the need for more time to problem-solve. And recognizing an alternative reason for your pet's actions prompts you to question whether or not that belief that you are never heard holds true in other circumstances too.

Consequently, you begin to reevaluate the idea that you are habitually ignored and strive to be more objective in your assessments and interactions. You start posing fundamental questions that hold the potential for paradigm and mindset shifts, such as:

> *Am I truly not being heard, or is it just noisy?*
> *Am I truly being disregarded, or is that person merely preoccupied with something else?*
> *Is my pet truly choosing not to comply, or does he simply need help going back to the basic building blocks of training?*

When digging deeper into beliefs we hold, it is helpful to ask ourselves whether our own experiences shaped each belief, whether it was inherited from our lineage or culture, and whether it is shaping a limiting mindset through which we view our interactions. This process of mindful introspection allows us to trade deeply ingrained limiting beliefs for mindsets that pave the way for personal growth, increased objectivity, and a more constructive perspective on life's interactions, including with our pets.

Beneficial Beliefs

Not all beliefs are limiting or holding us back. In fact, some can be positive forces for change. Beneficial beliefs facilitate connection, vitality, enrichment, and new outcomes. For instance, the belief *I can achieve anything I set my mind to* creates a mindset that inspires us to tackle challenges head-on, encouraging a can-do attitude, whether in life more generally or when training our pets. Ultimately, it can foster experiences of closeness, collaboration, and shared accomplishments.

Another beneficial belief is *I welcome new experiences in my life*. It opens the door to self-discovery, inviting us to embrace change and explore new aspects of our relationships and worldview. When applied to our connection with our pets, this mindset promotes adaptability, personal growth, and transformation in our lives and the lives of our furry companions.

So, let's dig into some mindset shifts that have the potential to create lasting behavioral change, allowing us to train smarter, not harder.

Triggers
& Mindsets to Shift

If beliefs shape our mindset, our mindset informs our approach to training our pets and the energy behind every interaction.

Pets respond to our words, physical cues, and body language, but also to our mindset. Although our mindset is not always intentionally or verbally communicated, it transmits in our energy and imbues every action or thought. And our pets are experts at reading these subtleties in our energy.

As we work on cultivating, adopting, and reaffirming empowering beliefs and mindsets that benefit us and our furry companions, we must be mindful of potential triggers that can nudge us back into less beneficial perspectives. The key is understanding that we have a choice and must repeatedly opt for beliefs and mindsets that uplift us and our pets, especially when feeling triggered.

Triggers vary in size and impact. Some are small, like concerns about unfinished chores, while others have more potential to disrupt our mindset, like deep-seated fears or navigating complex family dynamics. The size of a trigger matters because it influences to what degree it has the capacity to shift our mindset from beneficial to limiting and, therefore, how we should approach it.

When it comes to smaller triggers, they likely will not create any significant or long-lasting shifts in our mindset and can be managed with simple solutions. For instance, the feelings of guilt that come with procrastination associated with a growing pile of laundry can be addressed by simply handling the chore.

But those more substantial triggers, like facing profound fears or complex family dynamics, demand a deeper level of thought, care, and mindfulness. The feelings and mindsets that stem from those can have a significant and long-standing impact on beliefs we hold about ourselves, our relationships, or our abilities. It's crucial to consistently choose an empowered mindset and leverage effective techniques to create lasting change.

As we adapt our approach to triggers, we should extend a similar understanding to our pets. Our animal companions face their own triggers and challenges, so it's important to tailor our methods with compassion and effectiveness, addressing these challenges with the appropriate mindset and techniques according to their scale and intensity.

With that in mind, let's look at important mindsets to shift when it comes to living with or training our pets so that we can create change from an empowered, energetic vibration.

Mindset #1

I am a pet owner >> I am a pet guardian. Outdated terminology like pet owner does not honor the partnership and the role that our animal companions play in our lives. Not only does it fail to acknowledge their sentient nature, but it reinforces separation instead of collaboration. Terms like pet guardian or pet parent are more resonant with the direction our view on pets and animal companions is headed. Using more mindful verbiage is just one of the small but significant ways to reinforce a more collaborative mindset.

Mindset #2

My pet needs to change, not me >> We're in this together. One of the biggest shifts in mindset needed in order to learn to translate our pet's behavior and train smarter, not harder, is to stop regarding the dynamic between us and our pet from a place of separation, hierarchy, or dominance. Instead, we should approach it from a place of connection, collaboration, and shared responsibility. If we are asking our pets to shift their behavior, we will have to make shifts as well, always stemming from the realization that we're in this together.

Mindset #3

I've tried everything and nothing works >> I have new tools at my disposal to support big shifts for us both. As a responsible pet parent, you've likely delved into countless resources and techniques to nurture your furry friend's well-being. You've read books, experimented with crates and puppy pens, enrolled in group obedience classes, and may even have enough puzzle toys to create a canine amusement park in your home. But despite your dedication, you have encountered a disheartening sense of stagnation. The truth is, while you may indeed have explored every avenue within the existing framework of pet training, today's society, culture, and our awareness as pet parents are evolving. And with these changes come fresh methods and approaches to interactions with our pets. By approaching training through the integrated lens of mind, body, and energy, we can leverage new techniques to elicit shifts in our pets' behavior and, by extension, in our own lives. By adopting this fresh outlook, you're equipping yourself with new tools to drive significant change for you and your companion.

Mindset #4

I want my pet to stop barking >> I want an environment where we all feel heard. When working toward change for yourself and your pet, focus on the outcome you want to take its place, not simply on the absence of that behavior. For example, when faced with a barking dog, it's common to think or say *I don't want my dog to bark anymore*. We are very quick to identify outcomes we do not want, but we are not giving our pet any energetic direction or vision of what we want *instead*.

Wanting the absence of a behavior or simply using the words *No* or *Stop* are non sequiturs. Rather than merely instructing him or her to stop, redirect and show your furry friend what constitutes a better choice in the moment and reward that behavior. By avoiding non sequiturs, having a clear vision for how our pet should behave instead, and giving them effective direction on how to get there, we create more intentional and mindful shifts in our pet's behavior and learn to become more specific in our broader goals and vision.

Mindset #5

My pet is stubborn or is acting out of spite >> My pet is trying to show me something bigger. Our pets tell us a lot about ourselves. By exploring our relationship with our pets, we can better understand our own motivations, beliefs, and attitudes. When our pets are doing things like having accidents right in front of us or looking straight at us while grabbing something they shouldn't, it can feel as if they are being defiant. But there is always a deeper underlying motivation for this behavior, which often extends beyond the immediate circumstance and echoes in various aspects of our lives. This shift in perspective brings us to the understanding that something more significant is at play when our pets act in these ways. However, the message is not always straightforward; sometimes, deciphering what we are meant to learn from our relationship with our pet is unclear. Fortunately, there are simple strategies to interpret your relationship with your pet, including interpreting what each nuzzle, cuddle, bark, or tail wag is telling you, which gets us to our next mindset to shift.

Mindset #6

I wouldn't know where to begin >> I have all I need to translate my pet's behavior. It is natural to question how we can decipher the messages our furry friends are trying to share. You may be thinking, *I have no idea what my pet is trying to tell me*, *I recognize I need to make changes in my life, but don't know where to start*, or *I'm too enmeshed to be objective about the dynamics at play*. In these moments, our Translating Beyond Behavior℠ process emerges as a valuable and practical tool. Its framework equips us with motivations, beliefs, mindsets, and themes mirrored by common pet behaviors. It provides the insight needed to take the first step in deciphering our pet's messages and digging into deeper levels of communication with our animal companions, ultimately enhancing our bond and shared transformation.

Choosing Empowering Mindsets

As we work with our animal companions, we are giving ourselves the opportunity to re-examine our beliefs and mindsets—whether handed down generationally, through pop culture, or formulated from our personal experiences. We can choose to keep those positively impacting us while changing those holding us back.

But it is difficult to clear out old beliefs and energetic clutter and lean into new, more beneficial mindsets if we do not fully understand what is at the core of a particular belief. Why do we have it in the first place? How does it pop up more broadly in our life? Why don't we need it anymore?

On our own journey of growth and transformation, understanding what drives, inspires, or scares us in order to either overcome or embrace it is a critical step in making more mindful and empowered choices that lead to lasting change. But first, let's dig into an activity that will help us communicate and affirm positive behaviors and choices.

Activity

CHOOSING A MARKER SIGNAL

When working with your pup, constant feedback is important, so developing a signal or word that marks the behavior for which your pup is being rewarded is helpful. A popular marker signal to use is a clicker, which makes a sharp, distinct, and consistent sound.

Although many trainers and pet parents use a clicker, I prefer a marker word instead because if you have a leash in one hand and your phone or a coffee in another, you don't have the capacity to use a clicker. The marker word I recommend is short and sweet: "Yes." You can use the word Yes to mark any desirable behavior or choice your pup may display. It is a short word, and dragging that "s" sound at the end effectively gets your pup's attention.

Whether reinforcing or shaping a new behavior, use the marker signal to indicate the desirable behavior and pair it with a reward. For example, if you are teaching your furry friend how to sit, the second his back end hits the ground, mark it with a "Yes" and give him a treat. If you are working on getting your dog to stop jumping up on you, let him jump on you and ignore him. The second he decides to land four paws back on the ground, mark it with a "Yes" and offer a treat.

Digging Into Motivation with Maslow's Pyramid

From all the information we encounter in our years of schooling, it's intriguing to consider which concepts linger with us over time. In my case, it was not historical dates or scientific facts, and certainly not how to solve complex math equations. Instead, what left a lasting impression, dating back to Ms. Hulley's fifth-grade class, was Abraham Maslow's Hierarchy of Needs. I vividly remember crafting meticulous notes in my notebook alongside the sketch of Maslow's Pyramid made with a pencil and vibrant hot pink gel pen. So, it's fitting that this theory became a foundational piece of my work with humans and pets.

Abraham Maslow was a humanist psychologist who first presented this theory of human motivation in the 1940s based on a hierarchy of needs. His theory explains that all humans have an innate desire to reach their fullest potential and become self-actualized but are motivated to meet their most basic needs before moving on to more complex ones.

Maslow identified universal truths that drive us toward reaching self-actualization, such as we all want to feel safe, secure, and a sense of belonging. We all want to feel creative and important. We all want to feel inspired, productive, and have a sense of purpose. We all want to feel seen, heard, and sought out. We all want to trust our intuition and insights and have a clear vision for our lives. We want to have faith in ideas, ideals, and beliefs and explore what is beyond our immediate reality.

Maslow's framework helps us understand what motivates and drives human behavior. And it's no different when it comes to our pets.

Just like humans, every animal companion needs his or her basic needs met. As we provide them with a sense of security, loving boundaries, obedience training, and mental enrichment, we can tap into our shared energetic connection. By better understanding the role they play in our lives, our pets are more fulfilled and closer to reaching their own self-actualization.

Before going deeper into exploring shared motivation using Maslow's theory as a framework, let's pause and acknowledge that this perspective is new, even if long overdue.

We are taking a big step by correlating our human needs to our animal companions' hierarchy of needs. We are acknowledging that our animal companions are sentient beings with the potential to not only help *us* reach self-actualization but seek self-actualization for themselves as well. Through our energetic connection, they assist us on our journey but are also progressing on their own path of transformation.

By ascribing to this belief, we finally give animal companions credit where credit is due. When we truly honor their contributions to our lives, we understand how far their influence goes beyond basic companionship.

Shared Motivation

If we can identify how our desires and motivations align, we can work together to transform any behavior, relationship, or pattern into a beneficial one. Since our pets mirror our energy, there is crossover between pet parents and their furry friends.

Uncovering, understanding, and leveraging shared motivation can be a powerful tool to shift behavior and create change. When two individuals' motivations are aligned—whether they be human or furry—truly powerful, effective, and efficient transformation takes place.

Let's dig deeper into Maslow's Hierarchy of Needs, also known as Maslow's Pyramid, to truly understand the common needs that motivate our behavior—whether furry or human.

MASLOW'S HIERARCHY OF NEEDS

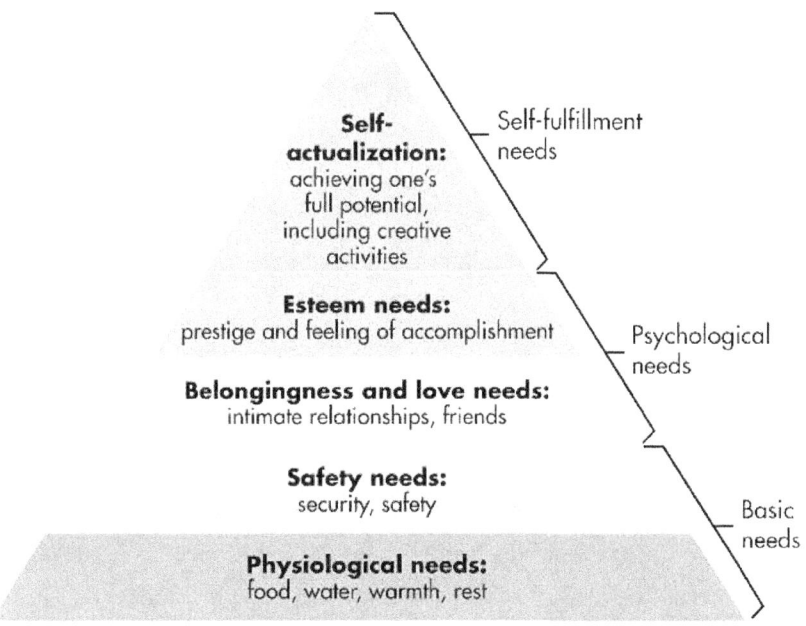

BASIC NEEDS. Physiological and biological requirements for survival. Basic requirements for survival include food, water, clean air, shelter, and sleep. Without these fundamental necessities, higher-level needs cannot be fulfilled. Simply stated, if you're worried about finding your next meal or where you will sleep, you're not really worried about writing your next big novel.

SAFETY NEEDS. The need for order, predictability, and control in our lives. Your next preoccupation is safety. We are all motivated to feel secure, including the desire for physical safety, financial security, and protection from harm. Most of us feel safest when we have predictability in our lives, are employed, and have adequate resources. Many of us also seek the safety of a community and people that will rally around us.

EMOTIONAL NEEDS. The need for interpersonal relationships, affiliation, connectedness, and being part of a group. Assuming our basic needs, comprised of our physiological and safety needs, are met, we bridge into the next level: our psychological needs. Our emotional needs include our desire for belonging, love, connection, and meaningful relationships. We long for friendship, familial bonds, and intimacy. Our pets' companionship and unconditional love play a significant role in addressing this need, contributing greatly to our emotional well-being.

ESTEEM NEEDS. Need for self-worth, accomplishment, and respect. This level of our psychological needs involves our desire to feel valued and appreciated, both by ourselves and by those around us. Maslow classified esteem needs into two categories: (i) esteem for oneself in terms of dignity, achievement, mastery, and (ii) the desire to be positively regarded by others, through respect, status, and prestige. This level of the pyramid entails building self-esteem, and confidence, having heroes and role models to look up to, achieving things you set out to do, respecting yourself, and earning the respect of others.

SELF-ACTUALIZATION NEEDS. Need for realization of potential, sense of purpose, self-fulfillment. Self-actualization is the aspiration to become the best person you can be. You understand your role in your family, friend group, community, and universe. You are forward-thinking, introspective, and aware of how you impact the world and the impact your world has on you. You're sophisticated, purposeful, intentional, and ultimately lead a well-rounded and fulfilling life, according to Maslow.

Our Pets' Hierarchy of Needs

When we look at the needs and motivations of our animal companions, there is a notable crossover between our needs and theirs. Building upon Maslow's pyramid, when we meet our pets' basic needs, provide security, implement loving boundaries, offer obedience training, engage them in mental enrichment, and understand and acknowledge the energetic role they play in our lives, our animal companions feel more fulfilled and closer to self-actualization.

Based on my observations from working with hundreds of clients and their pets, I've identified how these parallels manifest in the lives of our animal companions.

BASIC NEEDS. Just as humans require food, water, and rest to maintain their well-being, our animal companions have the same basic physiological needs. Ensuring their bodies are functioning optimally and they have their basic needs met is a fundamental responsibility for pet parents.

SAFETY NEEDS. Safety for our animal companions encompasses shelter and a sense of being part of a pack. This concept of a pack may not involve socialization or emotional fulfillment as it does for humans, but it represents safety and protection in numbers. Pets thrive when they feel secure within a structured pack environment.

EMOTIONAL NEEDS. Our animal companions' needs for love and belonging are met through traditional training and exercise. Engaging in activities like hiking, playing, and obedience training fosters a sense of love, acceptance, and belonging to their human pack.

ESTEEM NEEDS. For our pets, esteem needs translate to the need for mental enrichment. We fulfill this need by intellectually challenging them through puzzle-solving, exploring new places, and giving them specific tasks. This elevates our training beyond basic obedience commands, offering mental stimulation.

SELF-ACTUALIZATION NEEDS. Taking the concept of self-actualization to the next level, we acknowledge that our pets, like us, have an innate potential for growth and transformation. Exploring the energetic connection between us and our animal companions propels both into a deeper understanding of one another, our shared purpose, and how we contribute to each other's personal growth. This energetic connection is not limited to dogs, cats, or household pets; it applies to any animal with whom we share an affinity or bond.

Extending Maslow's theory to include our animal companions' shared needs and motivation is instrumental in effectively interpreting and managing our pets' behavior and creating lasting change for ourselves and our animal companions. However, if behavioral issues such as barking, nipping, accidents, or separation anxiety persist, it's critical to dig deeper into the energetic factors driving these behaviors.

Let's look at how we can use our pets' behaviors to learn more about broader energetic themes affecting our lives and pets, using the Chakra System as a helpful overlay to motivation.

Energetic Overlay
The Chakra System

Where Maslow's theory gives us a helpful interpretation of our physiological and psychological needs, the Chakra System helps us understand the emotional overlay and energetic theme driving our motivations.

As we read about Maslow's theory, some of us familiar with the chakras may already have started drawing parallels to Maslow's hierarchy and universal themes represented by each of our chakras. And that's no accident. Whether for us or our pets, every motivation has a physical, psychological, and energetic component.

The Chakra System is a great cheat sheet to help us identify the energetic factor behind every motivation because all of us, including our animal companions, have seven major chakras. Our animal companions' chakras systems mirror ours physically and energetically, making them a valuable tool to understand the emotional themes our pets are reflecting.

So, let's dig into chakras and how they can be used to better understand ourselves and our animal companions.

Digging into the Chakra System

Chakra is a Sanskrit word that translates to *spinning wheel*. These spinning energy centers through which life force energy flows play a vital role in our physical and emotional well-being. Each chakra relates to specific aspects of our body and a particular emotional state, representing universal themes.

Universal themes are archetypical emotional experiences rooted in our deepest shared desires and motivations. Examples include themes Maslow identified, like Safety, Belonging, and Self-Worth. Although circumstances and the emotional tone surrounding a theme can vary from person to person, the energetic essence of the theme is universally relatable.

When disappointment, denial, or challenging life experiences hinder the flow of energy in a chakra, it can create blockages that show up as physical manifestations in our body, as challenging emotions, or limiting mindsets about situations, relationships, or ourselves.

However, when immersed in these physical or emotional challenges, pinpointing the root cause is often difficult because the discomfort of the experience causes us to lose perspective and objectivity.

This is where our animal companions come into the picture. As we discussed in previous chapters, by reflecting our energetic terrain, our pets guide us to identify and deal with the core issues.

For example, if we notice our pet barking and lunging during walks, we can safely extrapolate that they are drawing attention to themes associated with the first chakra of Safety or Security, which are likely playing out in other areas in our lives beyond our on-leash experiences with our furry friend.

This is why it is helpful to understand each chakra, where it is located in our bodies, and its corresponding themes. They provide valuable clues as to what may be shaping our physical or emotional experience. So, let's explore the seven major chakras and the physical and energetic aspects each energy center governs.

7 Major Chakras Overview

Chakras represent various aspects of human experience and energy flow. Understanding their attributes can help achieve balance and harmony in our lives.

First Chakra (Root Chakra). Located at the base of the spine, it governs the lower body, including the legs, feet, and colon. Universal themes associated with it include survival, security, stability, grounding, physical health, basic needs, and connection to one's surroundings.

Second Chakra (Sacral Chakra). Positioned in the lower abdomen, about two inches below the navel. It governs the reproductive and urinary systems. Universal themes linked with it encompass balance, duality, sexuality, emotions, sensuality, and service.

Third Chakra (Solar Plexus Chakra). Found in the upper abdomen, just below the ribcage. Organs governed by it include the digestive system, liver, gallbladder, and adrenal glands. Universal themes associated with this chakra involve personal power, self-esteem, confidence, drive, creativity, and inspiration.

Fourth Chakra (Heart Chakra). Centered in the chest, near the heart, it governs the heart and lungs. Universal themes linked with it encompass love, compassion, forgiveness, empathy, intimate relationships, and the ability to give and receive love.

Fifth Chakra (Throat Chakra). Located in the throat and neck area, it governs the thyroid and parathyroid glands, as well as the vocal cords, throat, mouth, and ears. Universal themes associated with this chakra involve communication, self-expression, truth, clarity, and the ability to speak one's authentic voice.

Sixth Chakra (Third-Eye Chakra). Positioned between the eyebrows on the forehead, it governs the brain, pituitary gland, and eyes. Universal themes linked with this chakra encompass intuition, insight, imagination, perception, vision, and inner wisdom.

Seventh Chakra (Crown Chakra). Found at the top of the head, it governs the pineal gland, brain, and central nervous system. Universal themes associated with this chakra involve spiritual connection, enlightenment, unity with the divine, and higher consciousness.

Balancing our chakras through various practices, such as meditation, energy healing, and holistic therapies, can help restore and maintain harmony in your physical, emotional, and spiritual well-being.

What we can expect when our chakras are in balance:
- Vitality and Energy
- Emotional Stability
- Physical Health
- Mental Clarity
- Healthy Relationships
- Spiritual Connection

What we can expect when our chakras are out of balance:

- Fatigue and Low Energy
- Emotional Instability
- Physical Ailments
- Mental Fog
- Strained Relationships
- Lacking Purpose
- Spiritual Disconnection

Animal Chakras

Pets, like humans, have chakras. Traumatic experiences, illness, environmental stressors, or even disruptions in their daily routines can influence their energetic balance. Emotional issues, such as anxiety or fear, or changes in their environment, like moving to a new home or a new diet, can affect their chakras. As sensitive beings, pets are attuned to the energy around them, including that of their human guardians. As a result, when one experiences chakra imbalances, it can often affect the other due to the emotional and physical well-being of pets and their pet parents being deeply interconnected.

And this is key because, all too often, we put off addressing habits, relationships, and mindsets negatively affecting our bodies and emotional or energetic states. Instead, we focus our attention and efforts on our busy schedules, careers, or friends and family. Until our limiting mindsets and habits begin affecting those most cherished and vulnerable—our pets—we can't seem to find the time or motivation to change what is holding us back in our lives. But as some of our most honest relationships, we will do whatever it takes to help our pets—even finally taking time for introspection and growth.

So that's where our animal companions are so helpful if we let them be. Their behavior provides insight to help us identify the energetic issue at the root of what we are experiencing with them, identify the energetic themes of the chakra that are out of balance, and clear limiting mindsets and energetic blockages so we can all vibe higher.

How specifically are the animals helping us, you might ask? Enter our proprietary process, Translating Beyond Behavior℠, that links pet behaviors to universal themes associated with each of our chakras. We'll be translating some of the most popular pet behaviors in the next chapter.

ANIMAL CHAKRAS

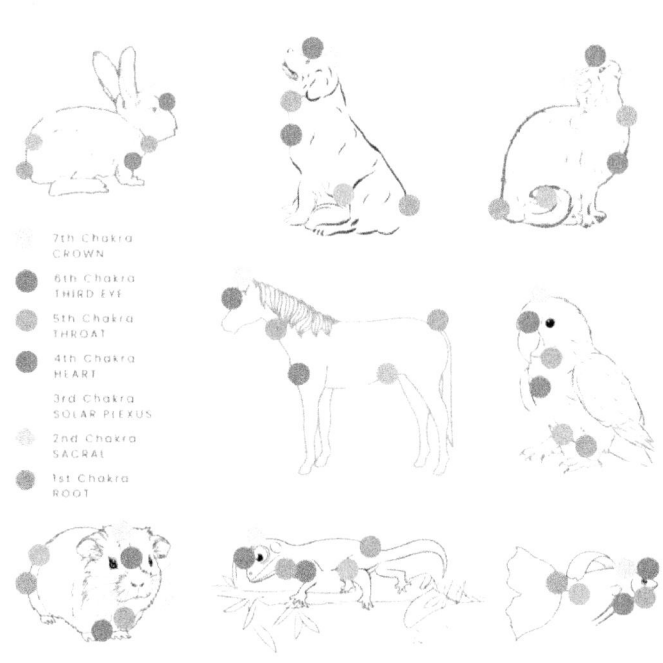

Our Proprietary Process
Translating Beyond Behavior^{SM}

Imagine a loving and collaborative relationship with your pet where you both feel seen and heard and thrive together. Imagine understanding exactly what your pet is telling you and what he or she needs to shift their energy and behavior.

When you learn to interpret your pet's signals, understand his or her motivation, and get to a place where you can quickly and efficiently translate your pet's behavior, you can create meaningful and long-lasting transformation for yourself and your furry friend. Ultimately, that means more time spent enjoying and valuing each other's company rather than focusing on simply "getting through" behavioral issues.

Our proprietary process, Translating Beyond Behavior[SM], which we will explore throughout the chapters of this book, is going to take us there.

This approach focuses on more than just correcting or eliminating pet behavior; it emphasizes understanding how everyday interactions with our pets can lead to transformation in all aspects of both our lives. We will transition from merely reacting to our pet's behavior to becoming conscious and mindful participants in the process.

If we accept the idea that our pets reflect our energy, we can draw parallels between their behavior and patterns in our own lives. For instance, if our pet displays leash aggression, it's worth considering where we may also be experiencing a similar pattern of lashing out due to feelings of insecurity or unsafety. Separation anxiety might prompt reflection on whether we're establishing appropriate boundaries. Guest reactivity could lead us to question our discernment in allowing others into our hearts and energetic space.

Translating Beyond Behavior℠ offers a roadmap linking common pet behaviors to underlying motivations and beliefs, which can also be tied to the energies of the seven major chakras. If we notice a specific behavior in our pet, such as housebreaking accidents, we can refer to its motivational and energetic overlay. This allows us to explore corresponding motivations, mindsets, and themes to find resonance. Once we identify one that aligns, we can begin to understand and shift the energetic pattern at the root of our pet's behavior.

We will still employ traditional training techniques because a solid foundation is important. But we will also learn how to translate the energy behind our pets' behaviors as we work on changing or reinforcing them together. Let's preview the process and behaviors we'll be exploring in this book.

OVERVIEW OF PET PRANA'S®
TRANSLATING BEYOND BEHAVIOR℠

7th Chakra   Missing pets
6th Chakra   Accidents
5th Chakra   Leadership
4th Chakra   Guest Desensitization
3rd Chakra   Unwanted Behaviors
2nd Chakra   Separation Anxiety
1st Chakra   Leash Reactivity, Resource Guarding

On-Leash Reactivity

Motivation: Basic needs of safety & survival

Energetic Overlay: Themes linked to the first chakra, including Support, Safety, Security, Victimhood, Confidence, Fear & Self-Reliance

Translating Your Pet's Behavior: Where can you build stronger foundations for success?

Separation Anxiety

Motivation: Emotional needs of belonging & connection

Energetic Overlay: Themes linked to the second chakra, including Balance, Boundaries, Separation, Worthiness, Guilt & Martyrdom

Translating Your Pet's Behavior: Where do you need to create loving boundaries?

Unwanted Behaviors, like Jumping, Nipping, Barking

Motivation: Esteem needs for accomplishment

Energetic Overlay: Themes linked to the third chakra, including Empowerment, Potential, Joy, Creativity, Accountability, Perseverance, Frustration & Self-Sabotage

Translating Your Pet's Behavior: Where can you step more fully into your power?

Guest Reactivity

Motivation: Emotional needs for love and belonging

Energetic Overlay: Themes associated with the fourth chakra, including Intimacy, Compassion, Devotion, Trust, Vulnerability, Courage, Loyalty, & Self-Acceptance

Translating Your Pet's Behavior: Where should you be putting yourself first?

Benevolent Leadership

Motivation: Esteem needs for prestige and respect from others

Energetic Overlay: Themes linked to the fifth chakra, including Communication, Authenticity, Truth, Assertiveness, Leadership, Being Heard, Empathy, Anger & Self-Criticism

Translating Your Pet's Behavior: Where do you need to use your voice?

Housebreaking & Accidents

Motivation: Esteem needs for being regarded by others

Energetic Overlay: Themes linked to the sixth chakra, including Acknowledgment, Regard, Perception, Vision, Expectations, Disappointment & Being Intentional

Translating Your Pet's Behavior: How can you lead a more intentional life?

Sick, Lost, or Transitioned Pets

Motivation: Self-actualization needs of self-fulfillment

Energetic Overlay: Themes linked to the seventh chakra, including Surrender, Transcendence, Spirituality, Purpose, Doubt & Faith in Moments of Crisis

Translating Your Pet's Behavior: Where can you have more faith in the bigger picture?

Deciphering Our Pet's Behavior

Remember, there is no one-size-fits-all answer when it comes to translating behavior. The prompts and ideas we will discuss in the next chapters will either feel right on, inspiring you to dig deeper to uncover more personal insights, or perhaps not resonate at all.

Like our pets, each of us and our relationships are different, but the goal of this philosophy is to translate what your pet's behavior may indicate for you. These tools are meant to empower you to be the expert and leader of your own life.

To most effectively translate and address our pet's behavior, our philosophy Translating Beyond Behavior℠ relies on the following principles and tools:

Context. Deciphering our pet's behavior requires that we pay attention to context. To truly understand their signals, consider the specific circumstances in which they exhibit the behaviors you would like to shift. Is their barking at other dogs on leash consistent or only on days you have stressful commitments? Does your pet only feel uncomfortable when certain guests enter your home or is their reaction to guests consistent? When accidents occur, where are they happening within the house? The location provides valuable context.

On the other hand, sometimes a bark or yawn is just as they appear. For example, your pup's yawn may be a relaxed release of energy if it's upon waking up or after a nap. But if it is outdoors on-leash and around triggers like new sights and sounds, it likely indicates mounting stress.

To effectively translate your pet's behavior, be attentive to their motivation, the timing of their actions, the location of incidents, your own mindset during these moments, and any additional contextual cues that offer insight into what your pet is trying to convey.

Energetic Coherence. Energy connects us all, and whether in the context of traditional dog obedience training or communicating with our animal companion, energy matters. The most basic and primal way to communicate with each other, especially with our pets, is energetically. Still, somewhere, it got forgotten as a basic building block of training and living a more connected life with our animal companions. To change their behavior, our pets require energetic coherence, which requires us to be clear and consistent in our voice, commands, body language, and energy. If we are saying *all is well*, but our energy is not reinforcing that, our animal companions will always go with the energetic message because energy never lies.

Traditional Training. Collaboration requires a clear path of communication and set expectations, so we need to build a foundation for open lines of communication with traditional training. Positive Reinforcement shifts unwanted behaviors by making desired ones more rewarding, whether via treats, affection, or attention. It is more collaborative and enjoyable because we are shying away from methods that are punishment-based. As part of the foundational training, we want to give our pups jobs to do, teach them loving boundaries, and help them be good decision-makers. Setting up consistent rules and expectations through positive reinforcement training helps them relax and become more confident.

Mental Stimulation. We want to ensure that we are working toward learning obedience commands to build rapport, paired with enrichment activities like games, adventures, and hikes for mental stimulation, which is critical to help your pet expend excess energy while building their confidence, self-esteem, and well-being.

As part of the new vanguard of pet guardianship, we no longer come from a place of separation. Instead of looking at our pet's behavior simply in terms of "naughty or nice" and being frustrated when they "misbehave," we can now become observers and identify the motivation and vibration at the essence of our pet's behaviors. When we understand the energetic reason behind their behavior, we can shift their behavior along with positive reinforcement training and shift broader energetic patterns in our lives.

Before digging into specific pet behaviors and translating how they may be reflecting our physical, emotional, and energetic state, let's review our final foundational concept: positive reinforcement training principles.

Principles of
Positive Reinforcement Training

Although our pet's behaviors have energetic components, it is critical that we first create a foundational language and understanding with our pets. We must teach them loving boundaries, give them tasks, and help them make good decisions. Building confidence and a common language is key for day-to-day operation and understanding. Only then can we move on to explore the energetic connections.

As we develop this common language through traditional training, we become more attuned to our animal companion's tendencies, body language, and thresholds, and they learn to better interpret ours. Striving toward a common goal builds a foundational level of trust on which to build stronger communication and connection.

Let's look at some key principles of Positive Reinforcement Training.

Sliding Scale of Rewards. A sliding scale of rewards is one way we can communicate to our animal companions good, better, and best in terms of their choices and behaviors. Rewards come in various forms. They can be treats, a toy, permission to jump up on the couch, and, of course, our love and affection. Harder tasks earn better treats or incentives.

Food as a Powerful Motivator. Your dog may enjoy cuddles and toys, but food is a powerful motivator when learning new behaviors. Food has the power to enhance a pup's ability to learn by raising dopamine levels in the brain and stimulating their natural desire to seek and earn the food, meaning that your dog is just as vested as you are in perfecting that new command or behavior. While shaping a new behavior, use high-value treats. Once the behavior is learned, lower-value rewards can be used to reinforce it.

Treat Roulette. When you are practicing commands, slowly wean out constant treating through an intermittent schedule of reinforcement. Ask for a command and give your pup one treat, then ask for another command and reward them with a toy or cuddle, and then jackpot the next command with three treats so that your dog never knows when the mother lode is coming and will work with you regardless of knowing whether or not you have food in hand.

Not All Treats Are Created Equal

Develop a sliding scale of treats so that you can best motivate and reward your dog for better performances and harder tasks. Imagine a scale from 1 to 10, with 10 being the most exciting treat.

1 out of 10: This could be a piece of your dog's kibble or a dry biscuit to leverage as a special "thank you" when rewarding your dog for doing a simple command like Sit without distractions.

5 out of 10: Usually store-bought, this treat should motivate your dog, but you have better treats on reserve. This would be used when teaching your dog a new command indoors or reinforcing an existing command in new surroundings.

10 out of 10: Typically chewy with a strong smell, this is the most special treat used when asking your dog to do something very difficult, like focusing on you outside around triggers or during crate training. Examples of common 10 out of 10 treats are string cheese or bacon.

What to Know Upfront

Obedience Training. Dogs, by nature, are pack animals. As you and your family become your furry friend's pack, he will look to you, the benevolent leader, for guidance. Obedience training creates a bond and opens up a clear line of communication between you and your pet so he understands and responds to what is expected of him. Training is also a great way to provide your furry friend with exercise, mental stimulation, and a "job" that builds his confidence and contributes to the pack.

Crate/Confinement Training. Dogs are den animals, even if sometimes we have to remind them of that. They normally take to crate training very naturally or once you create a positive association with it. Crates and playpens are useful in a variety of situations. If you have a new dog or puppy, you can use a crate or confinement area to limit access to the house until she learns all the house rules, like what she can and can't chew on and where she can and can't eliminate. During adolescence, it helps reinforce loving boundaries. In adulthood, it provides a safe place to rest and replenish, free from distractions or interruptions. A crate or playpen will also allow you to safely take your puppy places where she may not be welcome to run freely, like a weekend at a friend's house or an overnight at a hotel. If you properly train your dog to use the crate or confinement area, she'll think of it as her safe place and will be happy to spend time there when needed. Just remember never to use the space as punishment.

Housebreaking. Setting a routine for you and your furry friend will help him know what is expected of him as he grows and develops control over his bodily functions. As a general rule, you should take your puppy outdoors or to the pad 5-15 minutes after eating, drinking, waking up, and playing. Monitoring food and water intake will help you better adhere to the rule of thumb, "what goes in, must come out," and predict when your pup needs to eliminate. When in doubt, take him to his elimination spot to give your pup a chance to relieve himself. Even if he doesn't "go," he will begin learning the path from various places in the home.

Socialization. Well-socialized dogs tend to be less anxious, more adaptable, and overall more relaxed. Puppies are most accepting of new experiences up to 12-16 weeks old. Socialize your puppy as safely as possible from an early age, using towels to protect her from direct contact with the ground and keeping her away from dog parks or other high-traffic areas if she has not received all her vaccinations. Help her learn through treating and positive reinforcement to be comfortable with many different types of people, environments, buildings, sights, noises, smells, animals, and other dogs. The wider the range of experiences you expose her to as a puppy, the more dynamic and comfortable she will be in a wide variety of situations as an adult.

Rules of Paw

- A tired puppy is a well-behaved puppy. Ensure she is getting a combination of mental and physical exercise. This will help her sleep longer at night and minimize boredom-based nipping, chewing, and barking.
- Develop a sliding scale of toys and treats so that you can reward your dog for better performances and harder tasks.
- Ignore or interrupt and then redirect behaviors you do not like, and calmly praise your pup when she makes good choices.
- Remember that "no" or "stop" is a non sequitur and that re-directive commands like "Look" and "Touch" are great to help your pup make a better choice in any given situation.
- Be sure to handle your puppy from an early age. Touch his ears, paws, tail, and snout in a way that a veterinarian or groomer might. Invite friends or family over to interact with your pup and have him get used to people other than you touching and holding him, making his vet and grooming visits less stressful.

Recommended Supplies

- **Toys.** Interactive toys like a Kong Wobbler, Busy Buddy Twist 'n Treat, stuffed toys, ball
- **Chews.** Bully Sticks (low-odor available), Flossies, Antlers, Nylabones, Rings
- **Food.** Talk to your veterinarian to ensure your pup's nutrition is balanced. A good rule of thumb is that the first three ingredients should not be byproducts. If you plan to change your dog's kibble, always gradually switch to another food.
- **Treats.** Natural Balance, Wellness Brand treats, Low-fat cheese, Lean turkey, Skinless chicken
- **Equipment.** Freedom No Pull Harness, Yuppie Puppy Harness. Always combine a light Nylon collar with a tag for identification and a 4-foot leash.
- **Products.** Chew deterrents like Bitter Apple Spray, enzyme-eliminating products like Nature's Miracle

For curated pet products and resources, visit the Resources page on petprana.com or scan this QR code.

Activities

LOOK COMMAND TRAINING

The idea is to get your dog to make eye contact with you on cue, making it easier for you to redirect her behavior or show her what you want her to do. This is great to combine with TOUCH.

1. Hold a treat in your hand, with your index finger pointing out.
2. Place your baited hand in front of your dog's nose so that she can smell the treat and you have her attention.
3. Slowly move your hand with pointed index finger toward your eye level until your finger is horizontally in line with it resembling a military salute. Your dog should be following your hand, interested in the treat.
4. The instant your dog makes eye contact, mark it with a YES or a CLICK if clicker training and treat your dog. If there are times your dog is not looking in your eyes, help her out by making a tutting sound to draw her attention.
5. Repeat this exercise 7-10 times until your dog is consistently performing the LOOK command.
6. Without a treat in your hand, add the verbal cue "LOOK," bringing your unbaited hand with pointed index finger toward your eye level.
7. When your dog makes eye contact, mark it with a YES or a CLICK if clicker training. Treat your dog for performing the behavior without baited hand.

BUILDING THE LOOK COMMAND

Wean out the treats first through delaying rewards and then via an intermittent schedule of reinforcement. Always reward better performances with higher-value treats.

Once your dog is able to perform the LOOK command without distraction indoors, practice the command in different places with different distractions (e.g., in an elevator, outdoors, at the vet).

TOUCH COMMAND TRAINING

The idea is to get your dog to engage with you from a short distance, making it easier for you to redirect his behavior or show him what you want him to do. This is great to combine with LOOK.

1. Hold your hand as if signaling "4", placing a treat under your thumb.
2. Place your baited hand in front of your dog's nose so that he can smell the treat and you have his attention.
3. Place your hand down by your side, creating a touch target for your dog parallel to your leg. Your dog should approach your hand, interested in the treat.
4. The instant your dog's nose touches your hand, mark it with a YES or a CLICK if clicker training and treat your dog. If your dog is not coming toward your hand, help him out by putting your hand closer so the smell of the treat re-engages him.
5. Repeat this exercise 7-10 times until your dog is consistently performing the TOUCH command.
6. Without a treat in your hand, add the verbal cue "TOUCH," bringing your unbaited hand down by your side, creating a touch target for your dog.
7. When your dog touches your hand, mark it with a YES or a CLICK if clicker training. Treat your dog for performing the behavior without baited hand.

BUILDING THE TOUCH COMMAND

Wean out the treats first through delaying rewards and then via an intermittent schedule of reinforcement. Always reward better performances with higher-value treats.

Once your dog is able to perform the TOUCH command without distraction indoors, practice the command in different places with different distractions (e.g., in an elevator, outdoors, at the vet).

Ready?
Let's Dig In.

Now, let's take a closer look at common pet behaviors and see what can be learned from them. For each, we'll be examining:

Shared Motivation based on Maslow's Hierarchy of Needs.

The Energetic Overlay based on the corresponding chakra and energetic themes.

The Mindset Shift so we can adopt empowered mindsets and create energetic cohesion, where our thoughts match our body language and training cues.

Translating Your Pet's Behavior[SM] so we can have a better idea of what your pet's behavior is mirroring in other areas of your life.

Training Basics to put it all into practice.

And remember, it is important that we recommit to empowering mindsets while training our pets. All too often, we focus on what's "wrong" vs. what we are doing well. Pet training requires practice and patience. Use positive reinforcement to reward desired behaviors, be consistent in your training approach, and provide ample opportunities for your pet to succeed.

If your dog is well-mannered or does not struggle with a particular behavior, take the opportunity to consider how the themes and beliefs associated with that behavior and chakra are having a positive effect in your life and parlay that success into other areas.

Ready? Let's dig in….

Part 2: Practical Applications

ON-LEASH REACTIVITY
& Building a Foundation For Success

OVERVIEW

Shared Motivation
Basic Needs of Safety & Survival

Energetic Overlay
First Chakra affecting Feet, Spine, and Adrenals

Universal Themes
Support, Safety, Security, Confidence, Victimhood,
Fear & Self-Reliance

Translating Your Pet's Behavior
Where do you feel unsafe or insecure?
How do you react to fear and lack of control?
Where could you be more grounded and present in your life?
Where can you let go of victimhood?

On-Leash Reactivity

On-leash reactivity is one of the most common and overwhelming behaviors for pet parents. Reactive dogs typically feel insecure—believing that offense is the best defense—so giving them jobs to do on-leash helps them relax and be more confident. On-leash reactivity invites us to explore our mindset around grounding, safety & security, support, fear, and victimhood. All these motivations are linked with the most foundational needs in Maslow's hierarchy of needs and themes associated with the first chakra.

What Is On-Leash Reactivity?

On-leash reactivity in dog training refers to a behavior exhibited by a dog while on a leash when they become overly exuberant, anxious, shy, or seemingly aggressive in response to certain triggers such as other dogs, people, or environmental triggers. This reaction can include barking, lunging, growling, or pulling on the leash toward another dog. Conversely, it can manifest as a pup being so anxious outdoors that he or she freezes or shuts down, stressed to the point of not accepting even high-value treats. This behavior can be challenging for both the dog and the pet parent to manage. Less serious but still requiring on-leash etiquette training would be zigzagging, pulling, or ignoring your guidance on leash. With patience and understanding of what motivates your pet's reaction, combined with collaborative training and desensitization exercises, your pup learns to remain calm and composed. This leads to safer and more enjoyable walks for both you and your furry friend.

Understanding and addressing underlying motivations creates lasting shifts. So, let's dig into what needs and themes may drive your pet to on-leash reactivity and how they reflect similar motivations and themes in your life.

UNDERSTANDING MOTIVATION

Any time you experience challenging on-leash behavior, or you or your pet suffer from any physical symptoms affecting the feet, spine, or adrenals, it is an opportunity to examine matters of safety, security, grounding, and victimhood. Consider how these themes may be playing out in your life with your pet or, more broadly, in relationships, your career, or other pursuits. Once addressed, you may find quicker resolution to the behavioral or physical manifestations you are experiencing with your pet.

Parallel in Maslow's Pyramid: Basic Needs of Safety and Survival

On-leash reactivity in dogs can be seen as a response driven by a perceived threat to their safety or well-being. Just as humans seek to fulfill physiological and safety needs first, dogs may react on leash when they feel their fundamental need for security is jeopardized. This can trigger a defensive response to ensure their survival.

Parallel in the Chakra System: First Chakra

Understanding and nurturing the first chakra can be beneficial in establishing a stable and balanced foundation for personal growth and development. Practices like grounding exercises, meditation, and reconnecting with nature can help bring it back into balance and foster a sense of security and stability.

Signs It's In Balance

- Feeling grounded and secure in one's life and foundational relationships.
- Having a strong sense of stability and self-preservation.
- Experiencing a connection with your physical body and surroundings.
- Feeling a sense of trust and safety in the world.
- Good health and vitality.

Signs It's Out of Balance

- Experiencing excessive fear or anxiety about survival and security.
- Feeling disconnected from one's body or detached from reality.
- Struggling with a lack of being present or feeling scattered.
- Engaging in excessive materialism or hoarding possessions.
- Feeling like a victim and a tendency to be listless or easily angered and reactive.
- Having physical manifestations of issues with the feet, spine, or adrenal systems in your pet or yourself.

Unique Themes Attributed to the First Chakra

Fear: Protects us from danger, but if imbalanced can lead to irrational anxieties.

Abandonment: Feelings of not being nurtured in early life, affecting one's ability to form secure and reliable connections in adulthood.

Survival: Associated with our primal instincts, such as fight or flight responses, influences how we handle environmental stress and threats.

Grounding: Emphasizes the importance of being rooted in the present moment and having a strong connection with our bodies and the physical world.

Formative Connections: Linked to our maternal bond, it lays the foundation for our sense of grounding and identity within our family unit and cultural context.

THE MINDSET SHIFT

In order to be most effective in shifting your pet's behavior, it is important to approach the training with an empowered mindset and energetic cohesion, where our thoughts match our body language and training cues. Otherwise, we create confusion and uncertainty for our pets with mixed signals, which can exacerbate the very on-leash behaviors we are trying to shift.

Mindset Shift with On-Leash Reactivity

Going from feeling hopeless, out of control, anxious, and at the mercy of what you encounter on your walk *to* grounded, confident, calm, empowered, and capable of redirecting any reactions to triggers without catastrophizing if things don't go well throughout the walk.

Mindset Shift in Other Areas of Our Lives

Going From Limiting Mindsets Like >>
Being Stubborn
Feeling a sense of scarcity, lacking in resources, or not being supported
Being fearful and insecure
Feeling disconnected from yourself or the environment
Having a victim mentality or shrinking to avoid becoming a target
Always feeling stressed and anxious

Showing up in limiting mindsets like:
I always have to fight for what I want to achieve or keep.
I will always have to suffer to get anything of value.
I am never supported in my ideas, pursuits, or finances.
I am not in control of what happens in my life.
I am always waiting for the other shoe to drop.
I am not able to protect or take care of myself.
I am on my own, so offense is the best defense.

Going To Beneficial Mindsets Like >>
Being self-reliant
Feeling protected, abundant, and provided for
Able to stand up for ourselves and our non-negotiables
Feeling connected and centered
Having a strong sense of self
Transmitting security
Being calm, confident, and assertive
Feeling in control not of what happens, but of being able to handle any situation and go with the flow

Showing up in beneficial mindsets like:

I have the skill, patience, and determination to reach my goals.
Solutions can be surprisingly simple and shifts come easily.
I am secure in my ideas, pursuits, and finances.
I attract positive support from others.
I have the ability to influence and take control of aspects of my life.
I can enjoy the present without constantly worrying about the future.
I am capable of protecting and taking care of myself when necessary.
I can rely on others to help when I feel overwhelmed.

TRANSLATING YOUR PET'S BEHAVIOR

What is your pet's behavior saying about you? Let's explore some of the major motivations and themes that resonate within broader aspects of our lives associated with on-leash reactivity and how these energetic components contribute to our pet's behavior.

Where do you feel unsafe or insecure?
How do you react to fear and lack of control?
Where could you be more grounded and present in your life?
Where can you let go of victimhood?

In what areas of your life do you feel unsafe or insecure?
Given that lashing out or shutting down on leash is a direct response to feeling unsafe, our pet's behavior draws attention to areas where we may not feel safe, secure, or in control. Safety isn't limited to managing our pet's behavior; it's a comprehensive concept that extends to our career, relationships, and well-being. On-leash reactivity is our pet expressing that they need us to anchor the energy of safety and security for them, which means we need to anchor it for ourselves first. However, odds are, we may find ourselves just as lacking as they are in that department. Whether we feel like we don't quite have our footing because we are between jobs, are feeling insecure in our romantic relationship, are experiencing a physical issue, or even coming to the end of a lease, these life events may be creating more unsafe, insecure energy than we realize.

Practical Insight: Realize that the feeling of safety and security is a multifaceted element that influences every aspect of your life, from relationships to job security. By focusing on feeling safe and secure in another area of your life, you can parlay that energy to address not only on-leash reactivity but also broader life challenges of your own.

How do you react to fear and lack of control?

To walk securely in the world, we must move beyond viewing it as a perilous place and find ways to ground ourselves in feelings of safety. Just like our pets when they face an unexpected trigger, like a skateboard across the street or another dog rounding a corner, we can misconstrue something unexpected to be a severe threat. When stuck in a disempowering mindset, we may perceive something minor as an existential threat, leading to anxiety and exacerbated reactions to triggers. A big challenge with shifting on-leash reactions is that we cannot control or predict the triggers around us. But when we feel confident to face our fears, we can be more mindful of our reactions.

Practical Insight: To manage on-leash reactivity, reflect on your own need for control in various life scenarios. Consider where else you feel or have felt that you must fight for your survival. How did you react in that situation? Was the need to fight real or rooted in perceptions shaped by past experiences or limiting mindsets? When you're making your way in the world, do you feel safe and protected or do you view the world as dangerous and threatening? Do you freeze, take flight, or fight when uncomfortable or fearful? Ground into new protocols to find your footing. Recognize that the world is inherently unpredictable, and by mastering your reactions to the unpredictable, you'll not only improve your pet's behavior but also develop resilience and confidence that applies to every aspect of your life.

Where could you be more grounded and present in your life?

It is difficult to project confidence and protection to others, including our animal companions, if we are not present and grounded. If we are multi-tasking, distracted, or our energy scattered, our pets will not trust that we are aware and present enough to protect them when they feel in danger, making on-leash reactivity challenging to address. Even simple habits like taking a few deep, grounding breaths will help center us so we can project focus and self-reliance to our furry friends.

Practical Insight: Establish simple daily practices that enhance groundedness and presence in your life. Begin your mornings with mindfulness to set a centered tone. Embrace moments of digital detox by unplugging from your devices at specific times, allowing you to engage fully with your pet, loved ones, or personal activities. These practices enrich your ability to be present and strengthen your bond with your furry companion.

Where can you let go of victimhood?
Embracing victimhood is a strategy often subconsciously employed to appear non-threatening and stay safe energetically. When in this mindset, we project vulnerability and insecurity and tend to expect the worst.

A victim mentality can hinder our ability to protect and support our pets when they need it most. When we fall into this mindset, we view the world as a dangerous and uncontrollable place where we are a target, similar to how our pets perceive the environment when dealing with on-leash reactivity. Our insecure energy makes our pets feel like they have to fend for themselves, and the behavior that follows is often reactive, assuming the mindset that "*offense is the best defense.*"

As we work with our animal companions, our pet will require us to embody an energy that is confident, protective, and reassuring, which compels us to be commanding, present, and significant. When embracing this empowering mindset, we signal to our animal companions that we are strong enough to take care not only of ourselves and our energy but of them as well.

Practical Insight: Perceiving yourself as a victim can limit your ability to provide protection and support to your pet and navigate your life confidently. Leverage mantras and be cognizant of using confident body language to shift your energy from victimhood to empowerment, both for your benefit and your pet's well-being. This transformation can help both you and your pet overcome on-leash reactivity.

ON-LEASH REACTIVITY TRAINING

Now that we've looked at what might be the underlying motivation and energetic overlay driving your pet's behavior, let's dig into training tools and techniques to help manage on-leash reactivity.

The Essentials

Attaching the leash to a harness instead of a collar is a safer option when walking your furry friend. It prevents injuries to their neck and throat, especially for excitable pups, pullers, zig zaggers, and breeds like English bulldogs that have restricted brachial passages. Look for a harness that attaches to the leash at the sternum to reduce pulling and opposition force.

During walks, treat the leash like an energetic tether. Your energy affects your dog, so aim for a sense of security and calm.

To set your pup up for successful walks, try randomly putting on and taking off the harness throughout the day. This helps reduce the stress that may be associated with preparing for walks, making the harness and leash less likely to trigger reactivity, whether in the form of anxiety or exuberance. Practice commands by the door, in hallways, and in the yard to build familiarity. Play calming music to create a soothing atmosphere, and if needed, consider natural calming treats during initial training. These can help take the edge off and be gradually phased out as your dog becomes more desensitized to triggers and more reliably focused on you during walks.

When dealing with triggers during walks, be watchful for early signs of stress or excitement in your pup, including yawning, one paw up, licking their nose, or a hard tail wag. If you see any of these signs, redirect their focus with treats or commands to avoid escalating reactions. Creating distance or body blocking can also help manage triggers and give your dog space to calm down.

Take charge of the experience so your pup knows they can rely on you during walks. Body language counts—keep your shoulders back and walk confidently even if you feel out of control. Equally important is quieting mental chatter or releasing any anticipation of stressful reactions to stressors during the walk. Keep walks shorter but more frequent, and always try to end them on a positive note. Be prepared with treats and commands, and communicate politely to others if your dog needs space. Taking charge of the walking experience, giving your pup protocol as triggers approach, and keeping your energy clear will ensure a safer and happier time for your pup.

Loose Leash Walking

The goal of loose leash walking is to have your pet walk calmly beside you without pulling on the leash. Follow these steps to train your pet to walk on a loose leash:

- Begin in a quiet, low-distraction environment.
- Hold the leash with a relaxed grip, allowing some slack in the leash.
- Start walking forward, using a verbal cue like "Let's go," "We're off," or "*Andiamo*" to signal to your pet that it's time to walk.
- If your pet starts to pull, immediately stop walking and wait for them to release tension on the leash. When they do, praise and reward them.
- Continue this pattern, rewarding your pet for walking without pulling and stopping whenever they start to pull.
- Gradually increase the duration and distance of your walks, reinforcing the behavior with praise and occasional treats.

Remaining Connected

The "heel" command teaches your pet to walk closely by your side. Here's how to train your pet to walk in a heel position:

- Begin with your pet on your preferred side.
- Use a verbal cue like "heel" and start walking.
- Hold a treat close to your pet's nose and position it by your side to encourage them to walk beside you.
- Reward your pet with the treat and praise when they maintain the desired position. Always give them the treat at your side so they realize staying in position gets them the reward faster.
- Practice walking in a heel position in short bursts, gradually increasing the duration before reinforcing the behavior with rewards.

Dealing with Distractions

While walking outdoors, your pet may encounter various distractions that can challenge their focus. Here are some techniques to help you manage distractions during leash walks:

- **Use Positive Reinforcement.** Whenever your pet remains calm and focused despite distractions, reward them with treats, praise, or their favorite toy. This helps reinforce their good behavior. Reserve higher-value treats for on-leash training.
- **Maintain Distance.** If your pet becomes overly excited or reactive to a particular distraction, create distance between them and the trigger until they regain their composure. Gradually decrease the distance over time, rewarding them for staying calm.
- **Redirect Attention.** If your pet becomes fixated on a distraction, redirect their attention to you by using a treat or engaging them in a simple command. Reward them for refocusing their attention on you. If necessary, use your body to block their sight of the trigger so they can more easily focus on you.

- **Consistency and Gradual Exposure.** Gradually expose your pet to different distractions, starting with less challenging ones and progressing to more difficult ones. Be consistent in your training and patient with their progress.

Troubleshooting

Giving Your Pup Space. We all can use a little space now and then. If your pup is overly exuberant or fearful of a trigger like a bike or other dogs, give him or her a little space. Allow your pup to get used to the sight of the trigger at a safe distance, reward their willingness with a delicious treat, and then walk in the other direction. Over time, you can practice getting incrementally closer and interacting for longer periods of time, always keeping the experience as stress-free as possible for your pup.

Commitment. Asking our pups to work through their fears during a desensitization session requires a lot of them, so we humans also need to show the same level of commitment. This includes sticking to a training plan, regardless of the time and dedication it may require.

Chanting. Chanting rhythmic songs during walks with pups, like "*Row row row your boat,*" is beneficial for a couple of reasons: 1) if you walk to the beat and pause or change direction at each stanza, it keeps your pup engaged and focused on you; and 2) the rhythmic chanting focuses your own breathing and mental chatter creating a present, grounded, and predictable energy your pup can anchor into. Think of a song or mantra you might use to better pace your furry friend on leash.

Keep Them Guessing. Not much gets by our pets. They know the route of their usual walk and tend to have a couple of places where they are reactive, come to a full stop expecting a treat from the local vendor, or simply shut down. If this is the case with your pup, mix up the path of your walk to avoid creating habitual pockets where they may choose not to follow your lead. Plus, variety is the spice of life, so keeping things interesting makes everyone's outings more enjoyable.

Additional Considerations

Connecting in Moments of Fear. Sometimes, it feels as if your pup has left their body because they are so upset and reactive in the face of a trigger. One of my favorite techniques is getting down on their level, lovingly placing one hand on their heart and the other on their back, between the shoulders, to connect back in via the heart. When you connect at that basic level and join your pup, sitting with them in their fear, you let them know they are truly understood. Then, once you have met them where they are both physically and energetically, you can help your pup move on, grounding once again in energetic clarity and the directed focus of traditional training. Always note that sometimes whispering can get your pup's attention more effectively than joining in on the shouting match.

So Far, So Good. Often during pet training, we tend to expect things to go wrong. If our dog is reactive on leash, we hold our breath and tense up as another dog approaches. This signals to our furry friend that we feel unsafe, ungrounded, and need protection, which tends to prompt a reaction from our pup. Instead, anchor into the energy of "So far, so good" to help relieve preconceptions of any given situation. These four words can help shift the narrative in our heads and create space for new outcomes.

Celebrating Victories. With on-leash reactivity, there will always be ups and downs, good walks and less desirable walks, so be sure to celebrate and acknowledge the small victories vs. expecting overnight success. It's also helpful to keep walks shorter but go on them more often, trying to end all walks on a high note.

CASE STUDIES

Case Study #1

When Pets Are Proxies for Unleashing Hidden Anxieties

When training our pets, we must honestly ask ourselves whether we are ready for a change. In Penny's case, her on-leash reactivity gave her pet parent the opportunity to vent about larger issues at home under the guise of a pet problem. Although she said she wanted improvement during walks, subconsciously, they were still serving a purpose. Let's dig into Penny's story.

Penny, a spirited Schnauzer, was part of a tight-knit, loving pack. But like every pack, Penny's family had its own challenges. Penny's father used alcohol to cope with pain from a long-unaddressed injury, leading to tension and unpredictability that created an insecure atmosphere at home. Penny brought that same volatility to walks. Penny was gentle and relaxed until another dog approached. Then, she would aggressively bark, growl, and lunge.

Penny's mom wished for her furry companion to behave better on walks, but there was a deeper, unspoken role Penny's reactivity played in her pet parent's life. Penny's barking and lunging on leash was not only a reflection of the volatile energy at home but became a topic of conversation and a way to connect with neighbors. They would lend a supportive ear when her mom discussed her experiences with Penny on walks. As they passed in the lobby, neighbors would ask about Penny's progress, sympathize with setbacks, and cheer on accomplishments, no matter how small. In her neighbors, Penny's mom found community and a safe space to verbalize her frustration with Penny's disposition, which would go from calm and gentle to aggressively reactive at the drop of a dime.

Penny's behavior was a proxy for her mom to speak about unspoken worries, fears, and anxieties in her marriage. Every time someone inquired about Penny's training, it gave her an opportunity to vent and share without explicitly discussing the mirrored complexities of her relationship at home. In this unique dynamic, Penny's reactivity still served a purpose for her mom, who subconsciously wasn't ready to let it go just yet.

Practical Insight: In Penny's case, the on-leash reactivity still played a role in the pet parent's life, eliciting sympathy, connection, and community. Sometimes, we are not ready for real change to occur with our pets' behavior or in our lives more broadly, and having control over when we let go of a particular experience provides an unexpected sense of security in our lives.

Case Study #2
Reclaiming Trust and Security After an Incident

This case study is a story of resilience, trust, and rediscovering a sense of safety and security, all with the help of loyal companions. Through intentional communication and trust, this pet parent finds her way back to a place of physical and emotional security.

In the heart of a challenging chapter, a pet parent reached out for guidance via an animal communication session. A kind and caring woman, she opened her home to a family member recovering from substance abuse. Unfortunately, as the days passed, the situation took a volatile turn as that family member relapsed.

The once peaceful home became explosive, leaving the pet parent feeling unsafe in her own space. Fearing for her well-being, she had no choice but to temporarily leave while she explored options to reclaim her home. The urgency her evacuation required meant she could not bring her dogs along, who remained at home without her for a few days.

During her absence, her two dogs, who were typically well-behaved, escaped through a broken fence and ended up in a confrontation with the neighbor's dog. This unexpected and unsettling event shook the pet parent's trust in her dogs and her sense of safety in her home.

When the pet parent was able to follow the proper eviction protocol and safely return home a few days later, the trauma of the past events left her feeling ungrounded and unsettled. And the once routine walks with her dogs devolved into an apprehensive experience.

Seeking a way to mend the shaken trust and rebuild the sense of security with her dogs, an intuitive pet reading with me revealed an invitation from her dogs—one that would serve as a turning point in their relationship.

They invited her on daily trust walks on-leash in their own backyard, an idea that initially felt unassuming but soon revealed its profound impact. These trust walks became a powerful way for the pet parent to begin rebuilding her sense of safety, trust, and control. As she stepped into this experience, these walks helped her energetically reclaim her space, property, and confidence in her furry friends.

Happily, the pet parent was able to feel safe and confident enough to resume regular walks with her dogs around the neighborhood, trusting that going back to the basics of on-leash training helped build a stronger, safer foundation for human and furry alike.

Practical Insight: Her home, once a source of distress, had become a sanctuary again, and her dogs, who had once been a part of the trauma, were now instrumental in her healing. This story reminds us that our pets can help us find our way and restore our sense of safety and stability, even in the aftermath of a traumatic event.

Activities

GROUNDING INTO NEW HABITS

Mindful Breathing. Incorporate mindful breathing exercises into your daily routine. Take moments to focus on your breath, inhaling and exhaling deeply. This practice helps anchor you to the present moment, fostering a sense of calm and presence.

Reduce Distractions. Identify common distractions in your life and take steps to minimize them. Whether it's turning off notifications on your devices during quality time with your pet, implementing time management techniques to minimize distractions at work, or creating a dedicated space for mindfulness practices, reducing distractions can greatly improve your ability to be present.

Mindful Walking. Practice mindfulness during your daily walks with your pet. Rather than letting your thoughts wander, focus on the sights, sounds, and sensations around you. Be fully present in the moment, connecting with your pet and the environment.

Body-Scan Exercise. Try a body-scan exercise to reconnect with your body and feelings. Notice any sensations, emotions, or thoughts that arise. This practice involves focusing on each part of your body, releasing any tension and stress while mindfully and intentionally connecting to your physical and mental state.

SIT COMMAND TRAINING

The idea is to get your dog to sit, allowing him to do things like wait patiently and safely on the sidewalk before crossing the street, say 'hello' to guests in a polite and appropriate way, or even show restraint in order to earn his food dish.

1. Stand in front of your dog so that she can focus, and you will be in a leadership position.
2. Place your baited hand in front of your dog's nose so that she can smell the treat and you have her attention.
3. Slowly move your hand over your dog's head and toward her tail.
4. The instant your dog's rear touches the ground, mark it with a YES or a CLICK if clicker training, and treat your dog. If your dog is not sitting simply by following your hand, try gently stepping closer to her as you move your hand from her head toward her tail.
5. Repeat this exercise 7-10 times until your dog is consistently performing the SIT command.
6. Without a treat in your hand, add the verbal cue "SIT" while doing the hand gesture.
7. When your dog's rear touches the ground, mark it with a YES or a CLICK if clicker training. Treat and praise your dog for performing the behavior without baited hand.

BUILDING THE SIT COMMAND

Wean out the treats first through delaying rewards and then via an intermittent schedule of reinforcement. Always reward better performances with higher-value treats. Once your dog is able to perform the SIT command without distraction indoors, practice the command in different places with different distractions (e.g., in an elevator, outdoors, at the vet).

Never push your dog's rear down to the ground, as this may cause him to resist and pop up. If your dog has had a history of/is a breed that tends to have arthritis or hip problems, check with your vet to see whether she is cleared to perform the SIT command.

SEPARATION ANXIETY
& Creating Loving Boundaries

OVERVIEW

Shared Motivation
Emotional Need for Belonging & Connection

Energetic Overlay
Second Chakra affecting the Reproductive System, Bladder, Kidneys

Universal Themes
Balance, Boundaries, Separation, Worthiness, Guilt & Martyrdom

Translating Your Pet's Behavior
Where are you subjugating your needs or over-giving to serve others?
Where do you rely on others to feel complete?
Where are you creating barriers vs healthy boundaries?
Where is your safe space?
How has the fear of loss affected you and your decisions?
Where can you let go of martyrdom?

Separation Anxiety

Setting boundaries for our pets is one of the most loving things we can do to keep them happy and confident. Let's learn how to set up a safe space for your pup, manage separation anxiety, and create an environment in which they want to luxuriate, whether you are home or away. As we translate our pets' behavior, separation anxiety invites us to explore matters of balance, boundaries, separation, worthiness, guilt, and martyrdom—all themes associated with the second chakra.

What Is Separation Anxiety?

Separation anxiety in pets refers to a behavioral response when a pet, often a dog, exhibits excessive distress, agitation, or nervousness upon being separated from their pet parent or pack. This anxiety can manifest in various ways, such as stress barking, whining, destructive behavior, soiling their crate, or other signs of extreme discomfort when left alone. It can be a challenging experience for both pet and guardian, but through desensitization and redefining what it means to leave a pet alone, we can help our furry friends become more independent.

UNDERSTANDING MOTIVATION

Any time your pet displays stress when away from you or his or her pack—or you or your pet suffer from any physical symptoms affecting reproductive systems, the bladder, or kidneys—it usually relates to matters of balance, boundaries, separation, self-worth, guilt, and martyrdom. Consider how these may be playing out in your life with your pet and whether they are contributing to the behavioral or physical manifestations you are experiencing.

Parallel in Maslow's Pyramid: Emotional Need for Belonging & Connection

Just as Maslow's Hierarchy of Needs highlights our need for belonging, separation anxiety in pets can be seen as a response mirroring that same deep desire for closeness, connection, and being affiliated with others. Much like humans, pets share an innate drive for connection and being part of a pack. Separation anxiety often emerges when they perceive a disruption in these crucial bonds.

Parallel in the Chakra System: Second Chakra

The second chakra plays an essential role in our emotional well-being and ability to foster wholesome connections with others. Cultivating a healthy balance with emotions, our attitude toward life's pleasures, and the give and take in relationships enriches various aspects of our lives, whether alone or in the company of others.

Signs It's In Balance

- Experiencing a healthy expression of emotions and feelings.
- Feeling comfortable setting boundaries and balancing your needs with others.
- Experiencing a healthy relationship between masculine and feminine energy.
- Having a positive and creative approach to life.
- Feeling comfortable with one's sensuality.

Signs It's Out of Balance

- Struggling with emotional volatility and mood swings.
- Feeling creatively blocked.
- Experiencing a lack of sexual desire or unhealthy sexual behaviors.
- Facing issues with boundaries in relationships.
- Experiencing issues affecting the reproductive system, bladder, or kidneys.

Unique Themes Attributed to the Second Chakra

Emotions and Pleasure: Closely associated with a healthy range of emotions and the ability to experience joy in life.

Manifestation: Rules our ability to birth aspects of ourselves into this world.

Sensuality: Linked to our ability to enjoy the physical aspects of life, including touch, taste, and smell.

Relationships: It plays a crucial role in forming and maintaining healthy, symbiotic relationships with others.

Adaptability: Governs a sense of flow, adaptability, and going with the natural rhythms of life.

THE MINDSET SHIFT

It's crucial to delve into the underlying motivations driving this behavior to create lasting shifts in separation anxiety. So, let's explore mindsets that might be behind your pet's separation anxiety and how they may parallel other areas of your life.

Mindset Shift with Separation Anxiety

Feeling compelled to sacrifice your needs in order to stay home with your pet and experiencing guilt when you put them in the crate or have to leave them *to* truly believing that independence training makes your pet more confident, dynamic, and well-rounded.

Mindset Shift in Other Areas of Our Lives

Going From Limiting Mindsets Like >>

Being a martyr, self-sacrificing

Overcommitting when should be setting boundaries

Sublimating own needs in favor of others

Feeling unworthy of taking up space, time

Feeling guilty and shameful when enjoying life's pleasures

Expecting to always feel depleted

Having no boundaries when it comes to giving up your time, energy, needs, or desires

Fearing loss and separation

Having an "either/or" zero-sum mentality

Attracting one-way and conditional relationships

Experiencing over-giving and issues with receiving or asking for things

Not feeling worthy of simply saying "no"

Showing up in limiting mindsets like:

I feel unable to create a rich and fulfilling life on my own.

I feel insecure when there's change to my family or routine.

I feel I need outside validation of my choices and decisions.

I feel guilty taking time for myself or to pursue my dreams.

I feel guilty living a fulfilling life if others are not.

I feel ashamed about my true emotions and desires.

Going To Beneficial Mindsets Like >>

Feeling worthy and deserving

Having a joie de viver, truly enjoying life.

Believing things flourish in your presence

Feeling surrounded by beauty and fertility

Being magnetic

Feeling fulfilled

Never feeling separate; always complementing

Attracting whole and nurturing relationships

Striking balance between receiving and giving

Having balance and harmony in viewpoints, emotions, needs

Showing up in beneficial mindsets like:

I don't need anyone else to create a fulfilling life for myself.

I adapt and thrive in new situations.

I don't rely on external validation when making decisions.

I deserve to take time for myself and to pursue my dreams.

I am worth investing in myself.

My happiness is not dependent on the happiness of others.

My needs and desires are valid and honoring them leads to personal growth and fulfillment.

TRANSLATING YOUR PET'S BEHAVIOR

Separation anxiety in our pets often reflects broader themes driving our own experiences and emotions beyond our relationship with our furry friends. Understanding these energetic undercurrents can help us address separation anxiety with greater insight and empathy. Let's explore some energetic themes associated with the second chakra that your pup's behavior may be mirroring.

Where are you subjugating your needs to serve others?
Where do you rely on others to feel complete?
Where are you creating barriers vs. healthy boundaries?
Where is your safe space?
How has fear of change, loss, or separation affected your decisions?
Where can you let go of martyrdom?

Where are you subjugating your needs to serve others?

Separation anxiety in pets can often mirror a broader theme of sacrificing one's needs, people-pleasing, or over-giving in various aspects of life. When our furry companions exhibit separation anxiety, it's often a reflection of our own tendencies to put others' needs before our own, even to the detriment of our own productivity or well-being. In this mindset, we find ourselves being in servitude vs. being in service of those we love. When in servitude, we are giving all of ourselves, depleting our energy. When in service, we leverage available resources, skills, and tools to empower and uplift our loved ones without detracting from our needs and boundaries. Separation anxiety prompts us to discern when we are *in service* (approached from a balanced mindset) vs. *in servitude* (rooted in people-pleasing and guilt around saying "no") and explore a healthier balance between the two.

Practical Insight: Setting up healthy boundaries that differentiate between selfless service and self-neglect empowers us to serve without compromising our own energy and needs. Take time to reflect and identify areas in your life where you may be sacrificing your needs for the sake of others. Practice creating boundaries around your time and energy without feeling guilty. Recognize that you can better serve others from a place of strength and balance.

Where do you rely on others to feel complete?

Pets with separation anxiety often highlight deeper issues related to codependency, worthiness, and longing in our relationships. Their anxiety may parallel our own longing for self-worth and companionship. This can lead to unhealthy dependencies because we don't feel that alone we can lead a fulfilling life. This mindset creates a desperation to stay close to that which makes us feel whole, similar to the anxiety our pets experience when we're away. This reflection encourages us to examine our feelings of self-worth and how they shape our mindset when it comes to our connections with others. A mindful evaluation can lead to more balanced and fulfilling relationships.

Practical Insight: Start by exploring your sense of self-worth and its role in your relationships. How much do you depend on others to feel fulfilled? What are you longing for in your life that you don't believe you alone can achieve? Are you relying on your pets and others to feel complete? Focus on finding balance in relationships, which can empower you to engage in healthy connections.

Where are you creating barriers vs. healthy boundaries?

When we are uncomfortable setting boundaries, we have the tendency to build barriers around ourselves instead. Putting up a barrier instead of a boundary is a drastic attempt at self-preservation. We fear that if we give an inch, they will take a mile. Setting up barriers is a coping mechanism because we don't trust ourselves to uphold boundaries. They keep us separated physically, emotionally, and energetically, resulting in isolation. Separation anxiety in our pets can prompt us to evaluate whether we are setting up healthy boundaries or resorting to unproductive barriers. Just as pet parents can struggle with setting boundaries during independence training, they may also grapple with imposing healthy boundaries in relationships and careers. This reflection encourages us to differentiate between protective barriers and constructive boundaries that allow for growth and connection.

Practical Insight: Begin by identifying areas of your life where boundaries are blurred or nonexistent. Rather than relying on rigid barriers that isolate you, focus on setting boundaries that preserve your integrity and support your well-being. Recognize the significance of effective boundaries in various areas of life, not just with your pet. Work on setting clear boundaries in relationships and career, and communicate your needs effectively. Practice saying "no" when needed, recognizing that it's essential to healthy boundaries.

Where is your safe space?

As we think about setting up safe and loving boundaries for our pups, consider how you have been creating a safe space for yourself and setting up boundaries in your own life. It is as important for you as it is for your dog. As we teach our dogs new behaviors and habits, it is always an interesting opportunity for us to re-examine how the theme is showing up in our own lives.

Practical Insight: Take time to consider whether you have a refuge, be it a physical space, an activity, or just time away for yourself. Do you have somewhere you can go to recharge your batteries and be alone with your thoughts? Do you have a safe relationship or space where you trust that people will not push or invade your boundaries?

How has fear of change, loss, or separation affected your decisions?
The fear of change, loss, being left behind, or feeling disconnected is often at the core of separation anxiety in pets. The same way our pets struggle with being away from us, a similar anxiety can drive our own decision-making. Our choices in various life situations can be influenced by the fear of losing relationships, loved ones, opportunities, or experiences. Perhaps we panic at the prospect of someone losing a certain image they hold of us, resulting in a loss of love or validation. Our pets' anxiety urges us to question how our own anxieties surrounding loss and separation influence our choices, from career decisions to navigating personal relationships. Reflecting on this fear can lead to a deeper understanding of its impact and the potential for personal growth.

Practical Insight: Challenge your fear of change, loss, or separation by reframing it as an opportunity for growth and a natural part of life. Embrace the idea that change—whether in your routine, relationships, and even in how others perceive you—can lead to exciting new experiences, opportunities, and personal development. Gradually expose yourself to manageable changes to build resilience, preserving aspects of your old routine and connections that are beneficial through activities like a consistent training routine with your pet or regularly keeping in touch with loved ones via video chat.

Where can you let go of martyrdom?
Separation anxiety in pets can reveal a tendency toward martyrdom in their pet parents. In an attempt to alleviate our pets' distress when left alone, we may overextend ourselves and sacrifice our own needs, activities, free time, and even well-being. And this tendency likely

translates to other relationships in our lives. When in the mindset of martyrdom, it is easy to fall into patterns of mirroring back that our needs are not as important as everyone else's and that we should drop everything we are doing to help someone else. It is a hard pattern to break because it tends to lead to external validation. Recognizing this pattern in our lives can prompt us to reassess our role as a martyr, teaching us the importance of finding a more balanced way to care for our pets and ourselves.

Practical Insight: Seeking validation through giving and helping others can lead to imbalance. Let go of the need for external validation through service. Prioritize boundaries around what you can realistically give to others, including your pets. Remember that prioritizing your own needs allows you to better care for your loved ones. Seek balance and be mindful of when you may be sacrificing your well-being unnecessarily.

SEPARATION ANXIETY TRAINING

Establishing loving boundaries by providing a safe space for your pup through a crate or confinement area can greatly benefit your dog's well-being. Not only does it help manage separation anxiety, but it's also useful for housebreaking and dealing with reactivity issues.

When you give your dog free rein in your home, they may feel the need to defend the entire territory, causing stress and anxiety. Dogs are territorial animals, which can lead to behaviors like barking at the door, reacting to hallway noises or guests, and being restless around you. Dogs who don't have loving boundaries at home often show reactivity on walks due to their anxious state from the start.

Using a crate or confinement area effectively communicates to your pup that they have a small, safe space within the home where they can relax, whether you're around or not. To make it a positive place, associate it with good things like treats and rewards.

Crate & Confinement Areas

Let's explore the difference between crates and confinement areas. Crates are enclosed spaces with a closed door, which can be stressful for some puppies. Confinement areas, on the other hand, offer more freedom and are ideal for situations where you can't release your pup regularly to eliminate, like during work hours.

Consider your lifestyle and travel plans when making a choice. If you frequently travel with your dog, crate training can be beneficial, providing them with a familiar and safe space in various locations.

When setting up a confinement area, you can use a doggy gate or a pen. Make sure either option has a doggy door for easy access in and out of the space.

Ensure the crate or confinement area is appropriately sized for your dog. Dogs prefer tight spaces where they feel safe, so avoid getting a crate that's too large. Some crates come with dividers to accommodate growing puppies. A good rule of thumb is to ensure your dog can stand up, turn around, and lay back down in the crate.

In terms of location, place the crate or confinement area in social spaces where the family gathers. This way, your dog feels part of the activities but in a secure manner. Avoid positioning it where your dog can see the front door, as it may cause unnecessary stress monitoring and obsessing over when you come and go.

Portability is also essential. You can move the crate or pen around throughout the day or bring it along when traveling to provide your dog with a familiar, safe space.

Creating Positive Associations

When introducing your dog to the crate or pen, create positive associations. Shower your pet with compliments when your dog chooses to be in the safe space and toss in treats to make the area more enjoyable.

Gradually increase the time your dog spends in the crate or pen and out of your sight. Tools like Reiki music, long-lasting treats, and chews like bully sticks or calming treats can help soothe your pup during independence training.

Remember, independence training is not a punishment; it's about teaching your pup to relax and be confident on their own. It's a crucial aspect of their development and well-being. Embrace the process, and give your dog a loving space to recharge and rest.

Giving Your Pup Incentives

- Use mealtime as an opportunity for independence training when your pup is hungry and enjoying her food.

- Place your puppy in her space with the food and close the crate or pen door while she eats. If she's not comfortable, leave the door ajar and progress slowly.
- Offer anything your pup values, like toys or treats, in her safe space to create positive associations.
- Leverage interactive toys and high-value treats for independence training to help your pup expend excess energy in a positive way.
- Associate your absence with delicious treats and fun toys, and remove them upon your return to maintain their appeal.
- Keep your pup entertained while confined to avoid boredom and anxiety.

Gradual Desensitization to Crate or Pen

- Sit quietly near the crate or confinement area for 5 to 10 minutes, then go into another room for a few minutes.
- Return and sit quietly again for a short time, then let your pup out of the crate or pen.
- Repeat this process several times a day, gradually increasing the time you leave your pup in the crate or pen and the time you're out of their sight.
- Once your dog can stay quietly in the crate or confinement area for about 30 minutes with you out of sight, you can begin leaving them confined for short periods and at night for sleep.

Troubleshooting

Timing. It's normal for your dog to whine or bark initially, but you should see a gradual decrease in this behavior during independence training. Typically, pups settle down after 12-15 minutes. If your pup is upset beyond that, the separation anxiety is considered more serious. Take note of how long your dog has been in the crate or confinement area when upset. Set them up for success by releasing them earlier next time.

Earning the Right to Exit. If your pup is barking or whining, wait for a moment of silence, mark it with a YES, and ask for a simple command like "Look" to earn the right to come out. In urgent situations, you can interrupt the barking with a clap, confident "hey," or a squeak from a toy to redirect your pup's attention to focus on you.

Attention. Avoid giving your pup excessive attention when they are released from the safe space to minimize the contrast between being confined and reunited with you. Showing excitement upon their exit from the crate or confinement area sends your pup the wrong message about independence training.

Additional Considerations

Managing Expectations and Building Boundaries. Whether it comes to our pets adjusting to the confinement area or crate or to ourselves upholding and being consistent with our boundaries, we have to be realistic. Just as we need to ease our pets into independence training and set them up for success by respecting their stress thresholds, we want to do the same for ourselves when working toward stronger boundaries. Especially in established relationships where others have grown to expect that we'll concede and self-sacrifice, it helps us to ease them into a new dynamic in our boundary-setting. And although, just like with our pets' training, we want to be consistent, we don't need to be rigid. If sometimes our response to a request is yes and sometimes no, that's ok, as long as we are not falling back into decisions based on guilt and people-pleasing. We can also set everyone up for success by communicating boundaries ahead of time. Letting someone know *"I am unavailable on Thursdays and Fridays"* helps them plan accordingly and prevents us from feeling pressured to revert to old habits due to the urgency of a request.

Support During Changes. For many of us pet parents, increased separation anxiety occurs when we have a big change to our pack. When we experience a breakup, a loved one passing, or even a longtime roommate moving out, we tend to lean on our pets for support. Beyond our emotional experience of feeling sad, vulnerable, fragile, or grieving, odds are, there may also be big changes to our daily routine.

As our pets read our energy and frame of mind, they often become more protective of us, leading to increased separation anxiety. In their minds, if they're physically away from us, they cannot ensure we are safe and well.

In these moments, continue to lean on your pets as you process your emotions and settle into your "*new normal*." As you work with your pet on independence training, remain mindful of your altered emotional state and how your pet may be interpreting it. Know that as you work with our animal companion on their independence training, they are helping you do the same.

Guilt. We often feel guilty when leaving our dog alone during independence training. These feelings of guilt around boundary setting are usually representative of a more extensive pattern for pet parents. Exploring the delicate balance between caring for our pet and fostering independence in our furry friend serves as a dress rehearsal to translate the same equilibrium in our personal relationships and professional life. As we navigate guilt associated with choosing between our perceived duties and our desires—what we *should* do vs. what we actually *want* to be doing—we understand that enforcing boundaries is as necessary for pet training as it is for personal growth. When we embrace the notion that asserting loving boundaries is an act of self-worth rather than a cause for guilt, we can navigate life's choices with increased enjoyment and self-awareness.

CASE STUDIES

Case Study #1

Bonds that Build Loving Boundaries

For many of us who have experienced conditional love or one-way relationships, we turn to our pets for that sense of unconditional love and completion. However, relying so fully on our pets to experience love rather than being fulfilled in ourselves first can create a sense of co-dependency, reinforcing the mindset that love must be constantly sought externally. When we believe love is conditional, habits and patterns of self-sacrifice and over-giving begin manifesting in our relationship with our pets. However, our pets are here to teach us that love is not contingent upon self-sacrifice and that, in fact, boundaries foster bonding, as was the case of Pepper.

When a client reaches out for separation anxiety training, it's often accompanied by strong feelings of guilt. This particular case was no exception.

From his earliest childhood memories, this pet parent had longed for unconditional love from a canine companion. After years of yearning, he finally felt established enough in his career to bring home a furry friend. Pepper quickly became the single, most significant relationship in his life.

Pepper's arrival was a dream come true, a lifelong aspiration realized. However, whereas the pet parent envisioned boundless displays of affection and an unwavering connection, reality unfolded differently than his childhood dreams. Instead of being gushingly warm and loving, Pepper appeared aloof and standoffish, yet still expected him to be consistently present and available. This was a particularly painful experience, as the pet parent looked to her displays of affection as an indication that she loved him. Determined to make Pepper love him more, the pet parent embarked on a relentless journey of self-sacrifice, believing it was the key to earning her affection.

In his quest to earn Pepper's love, he dismantled his own boundaries piece by piece, leaving little room for enjoyment in his life. Even the simple acts of leaving the apartment to grab a coffee or enjoying a meal were tainted by guilt, as he felt compelled to divert all his attention and care toward Pepper.

This pet parent truly believed that erasing boundaries would enhance their connection. Instead, it created a void and pushed Pepper further away. Unbeknownst to him, the pup yearned for boundaries, the kind that would convey love, care, and structure. As the pet parent neglected his own needs and regard for himself, Pepper mirrored back and reciprocated this diminishing energy.

Upon reflection during our session, the pet parent realized that this attempt to suppress his own needs in order to gain love extended beyond his relationship with Pepper. It painted a broader picture that traced back to his upbringing in a strict, traditional household. It was a theme born from limiting beliefs formed as a child, perceiving that he received more love and approval from his parents when his needs took a back seat to their desires. He felt the conditional approval of his parents was based on the degree to which he diminished his own needs and desires in favor of upholding theirs. With this realization the pet parent was able to reframe the mindset he held regarding our training protocol and worked toward a more balanced and fulfilling dynamic with Pepper where both of their needs were equally considered and met. Not only did he build a healthier, more rewarding relationship with Pepper, but he parlayed that same mindset of implementing loving boundaries with the employees at his company.

Practical Insight: While equating self-sacrifice with love is a difficult mindset to change, this case teaches us that boundaries can, in fact, strengthen the bonds we share. Just as in the case of Pepper, our furry friends often seek the comfort of boundaries. These lessons from our pets translate into other aspects of our lives, reinforcing that loving boundaries are not a separation but can create more fulfilling and loving relationships.

Case Study #2

A Journey to Trust and Self-Worth

A rescue pup's struggle with separation anxiety served as a mirror, reflecting his human's unexamined mindset regarding her own worthiness. By delving into the pet parent's past and leveraging a cherished teddy bear, we unearthed a shared mindset that lay at the core of the pup's anxiety.

When a pet parent reached out to me regarding her dog's separation anxiety, it marked the beginning of a transformative journey for her. Although we were on opposite coasts, our virtual training session bridged the gap, and we set out to address this challenge together.

Our initial approach involved a series of desensitization exercises to alleviate the pup's anxiety when separated from her. I was able to watch his reactions virtually as she slipped out of the room, which allowed me to see that he was still struggling with separation and the training methods we were using. As we delved deeper into our session, it became apparent that a more mindful solution was needed, one that would address what was truly at the core of his separation anxiety.

As we shifted the focus of our training, I instructed the pet parent to select an item of personal significance. She chose a beloved teddy bear off her bed, a treasured childhood companion. With the teddy bear in hand, I asked her to share with her dog through a heartfelt demonstration how much she valued this sentimental memento, communicating its profound significance in her life.

The next step was pivotal. I had the pet parent ask her dog to watch over and guard the teddy bear in her absence. As she stepped out of sight, something truly remarkable occurred. For the first time, the dog felt a profound sense of purpose. He picked up the teddy bear and placed it within his dog bed, adopting the role of its faithful guardian. With unwavering dedication—and more comfortably and calmly than in previous exercises—he patiently awaited his pet parent's return.

Energetically, this transformative moment tapped into the core of the dog's separation anxiety. It became clear that his anxiety was not rooted in a fear of missing out on an adventure or a desire to keep his pet parent in sight at all times. Instead, the anxiety he felt when separated from his pet parent was based in feelings of unworthiness, believing he wasn't significant enough to merit his pet parent's return. This revelation was nothing short of heart-wrenching, particularly considering how deeply the pet parent cherished her beloved dog.

At its essence, this belief that she would return for a valuable item but perhaps not for him at the heart of the dog's separation anxiety mirrored the feelings of unworthiness that the pet parent had experienced during her own childhood, where she never felt valued or a priority in her family unless she was actively contributing or helping in some way. The echoes of this past experience had permeated her present relationships and interactions, subtly shaping her approach to life and romantic relationships. Through the mirroring of her beloved furry friend, she was able to revisit feelings she experienced as a child, and now, in the role of a parent, she truly understands how much a child is cherished and valued without conditions—whether human or furry.

Practical Insight: This touching case exemplifies how our pet's anxieties can help us heal deep-seated beliefs around self-worth. The teddy bear became a tangible connection to the pet parent and a source of reassurance, making the pet feel less anxious about the separation. Importantly, this interaction also prompted the pet parent to reflect on her own sense of worth and how it shaped her interactions with the world.

Activities

CREATING A PEACEFUL SPACE FOR YOUR PET

Music Soothes the Beast. Music helps set the tone and drown out any ambient noises or sounds that can set off or stress your pup. Rather than leaving on the news, Animal Planet, cartoons, or classical music, which can be overstimulating or jarring with its crescendos, try soothing spa-like Reiki healing sounds to create a tranquil environment where your pup wants to luxuriate. YouTube is a great place to find loops that last for hours at a time.

D.A.P. Spray. Dog-appeasing pheromones (DAP) mimic the comforting pheromones a pup's mother emits during nursing and are used to help keep your pup calm in stressful situations. DAP comes as a spray, a diffuser, or a wearable collar. Spritz the DAP Spray on a favorite blanket or a Heartbeat Snuggle Toy to help your pup relax overnight or while you are away. For some pups, it makes a noticeable difference; for others, it is less effective, but as an all-natural resource, there is little downside to trying it.

SHOWER OF COMPLIMENTS

The idea is to teach your pet that when he goes into his crate or confinement area, it doesn't mean he'll be left alone. Rather, he will receive your attention and positive reinforcement.

Whether in the crate or confinement area, make sure there's a little door or space where your pup can go in and out on his own.

If you happen to be sitting on the couch watching TV with the crate door open and your dog decides to go in, initiate the Shower of Compliments. When you see him going in, calmly tell him what a handsome boy he is, how he made a great choice, and how he is so smart. Keep gushing while your pup chooses to stay in his safe space.

The second he decides to walk out, ignore him. If he turns around and decides to step back into his space, then the Shower of Compliments commences again.

For the Shower of Compliments to be successful, ensure that your energy reflects the energy you want to see during independence training. Be mindful of your tone, bring down your energy level, and let him know he is doing a great job. If he is calmly lying down and you're using an excitable tone, he will meet you at your energetic vibration and pop right up and hop toward you, which is the opposite of the behavior you were praising. Therefore, it is important that you model and mirror back the energy you want to see through a calm, soothing tone.

TREATS FROM HEAVEN

The idea is to gradually desensitize your pet to the crate or confinement area by creating a positive association with it. Reward time spent calmly in his safe space by tossing treats, starting with very regular intervals and gradually increasing the time between treats.

If your pup is hanging near or in a crate or confinement area, find a nearby seat within throwing distance. Bring with you a jar of kibble or treats and either a book, your computer, or turn on the television.

If your dog decides to go into his crate, pen, or confinement area, toss a treat in his safe space. You want to avoid your pup making the connection that the treats are coming from you. Otherwise, you are reinforcing the value of your presence. Instead, we want him to think that every time he steps in this space, treats literally fall from the sky.

So, any time he decides to walk into his safe space, toss a "treat from heaven." If your pup is working on his independence training with the door closed, and he's being quiet, toss in a treat and extend how long before you toss the next one. In the beginning of independence training, you might be very generous and regular with the treats, but as your pup gets more comfortable, work up to the point where you're tossing in an occasional reward just to reinforce the behavior.

DOWN COMMAND TRAINING

The idea is to get your dog to lie down, allowing him to say 'hello' to guests politely and appropriately or even show restraint to earn his food dish.

1. Gesture for your dog to SIT without using the verbal cue (hand gesture only).
2. Put a treat in the palm of your hand and close it, keeping your index finger pointed. Let your dog smell the treat so that he is focused on you.
3. Slowly bring your baited hand from your dog's nose into his chest and down to the ground so that he will follow your pointed index finger, coaxing him into a DOWN position. If it doesn't work, try it again.
4. The instant your dog's belly touches the ground, mark it with a YES or a CLICK if clicker training and treat your dog. If your dog is not lying down simply by following your hand, start shaping the behavior by treating him when elbows are bent, close to lying down.
5. Repeat this exercise 7-10 times until your dog consistently performs the DOWN command.
6. Without a treat in your hand, gesture for your dog to go DOWN. Straighten up an inch before using the marker word YES and treat and praise him for performing the behavior without a baited hand. If your dog pops up as you inch up, try again.
7. Work your way up into a standing position inch by inch until your dog responds to you in a standing position, emphatically pointing to the ground. Once he is, add the verbal cue "DOWN" while doing the hand gesture.

BUILDING THE DOWN COMMAND

Wean out the treats first through delaying rewards and then via an intermittent schedule of reinforcement. Always reward better performances with higher-value treats. Once your dog can perform the

DOWN command without distraction indoors, practice the command in different places with different distractions (e.g., in an elevator, outdoors, at the vet).

RELAX COMMAND TRAINING

The idea is to condition your dog to relax on a mat so that the behavior can be transferred as needed on cue in stressful situations, such as guests entering your home or encountering triggers outdoors.

1. In a calm environment, introduce your dog to the mat. As your dog approaches the mat, click or mark it with a YES and toss a treat on the mat.
2. Reward your dog as she displays calm behavior on the mat. This includes marking and rewarding for relaxed body language, such as sniffing, loose ears and tail, relaxed tongue, sighing, and sleepy eyes. Also, reward for elbows bending and/or body lowering toward the mat.
3. The second your dog chooses to SIT on the mat, mark it with a YES and jackpot.
4. The second your dog chooses to LAY DOWN on the mat, mark it with a YES and jackpot, as this is the ultimate desired behavior.
5. Once your pup is lying on the mat, ask for a TOUCH and remove the mat for a few seconds.
6. Re-introduce the mat and repeat the above process, with the objective that, ultimately, your dog will LAY DOWN on the mat once it comes out. (Once your dog is reliably lying down on the mat when it is introduced, you may add the verbal cue "GO TO MAT.")
7. Once your dog is on the mat in a DOWN position, begin by taking three deep breaths, mark with a YES, and reward your dog if she displays any signs of relaxation, including a sigh.
8. Begin massaging your dog in a clockwise gesture on her ears, at the base of her jaw, and then in long motions from her head to her tail. As you do this, make a soothing "Shhhh" sound. As you massage your pup, focus on her breathing and hold in your mind's eye instances where your dog made you proud and happy and was calm and relaxed.

9. Mark and reward signs of relaxation such as blinking, stretching, sleepy eyes, sighing, etc. As your dog begins to reliably offer these relaxation behaviors when she sees the mat, add the verbal cue "RELAX."
10. Once the exercise is done, ask for a TOUCH, toss a treat off the mat, and remove it.

BUILDING THE RELAX COMMAND

First, practice this exercise when your dog is tired and the house is calm. Feel free to create a spa-like experience with relaxing music and candles. Consider using lavender or bach flower essences for particularly anxious dogs during the massage.

Keep sessions short and frequent, always ending on a success. If your dog is getting excitable every time you use the marker word YES, try using a softer, calmer tone.

Once your dog can perform the RELAX command without distractions on the mat, practice the command indoors with different distractions (e.g., around a favorite toy, with a knock at the door, etc., always ensuring you are slowly building toward the more stressful triggers). Then, once accomplished indoors, practice the command in different places with different distractions outside the house.

BARKING, NIPPING, JUMPING
& Stepping into Your Power

OVERVIEW

Shared Motivation
Esteem Needs for Accomplishment

Energetic Overlay
Third Chakra affecting Skin, Pancreas, Liver, Stomach

Universal Themes
Empowerment, Potential, Joy, Creativity, Accountability, Perseverance, Frustration & Self-Sabotage

Translating Your Pet's Behavior
Where are you disempowering yourself?
What projects are you putting off?
Where are you feeling stuck?
Where can you let go of self-sabotage?

Unwanted Behaviors

Learn strategies to manage or prevent unwanted behaviors, like jumping, boredom barking, or nipping. Discover how they may invite us to manage our energy and step more fully into our own power. As we translate our pet's behaviors, explore matters of personal power, taking action & responsibility, frustration, and self-sabotage—all themes associated with the third chakra and managing unwanted behaviors.

What Are Unwanted Behaviors?

Unwanted behaviors in pet training include boredom and attention barking, jumping, nipping, and excessive chewing, and are primarily driven by factors like excess energy, lack of mental stimulation, or a desire for attention. These behaviors can be disruptive and frustrating for pet parents, leading to a need for intervention and redirection. Stimulating activities and positive reinforcement techniques can very effectively redirect and discourage these unwanted behaviors.

UNDERSTANDING MOTIVATION

Any time your pet engages in unwanted behaviors—or you and your pet suffer from physical symptoms affecting the skin, pancreas, liver, or stomach—it is an opportunity to explore matters of empowerment, potential, joy, creativity, accountability, frustration, and self-sabotage. Consider how these factors may influence your pet's conduct and how they relate to your own feelings about their behavior.

Parallel in Maslow's Pyramid: Esteem Needs for Accomplishment

Just as Maslow's Hierarchy of Needs highlights our need for accomplishment, our pet's unwanted behaviors reflect their desire to funnel their energy into a productive pursuit. Much like humans, pets also seek to fulfill their esteem needs, which are met through achieving training goals, having tasks to do, and engaging in mentally stimulating activities. Barking, nipping, or jumping express frustration or a last-resort effort when they cannot achieve their goals more constructively. Persistence in these behaviors can also signal that we may not be fulfilling our own potential.

Parallel in the Chakra System: Third Chakra

Engaging in activities that boost accountability and help achieve personal goals can help bring the third chakra into alignment, leading to a more accomplished and inspired life.

Signs It's In Balance

- Feeling confident and having a strong sense of impact.
- Being decisive.
- Able to set and achieve personal goals.
- Having a balanced sense of accountability and perseverance.
- Feeling productive and accomplished.

Signs It's Out of Balance

- Struggling with low self-esteem.
- Experiencing difficulty in making decisions.
- Procrastination, lack of focus, and stagnation.
- Frustration with self, experiences, and situations.
- Suffering from digestive issues or other physical problems in the abdominal region or skin.

Unique Themes Attributed to the Third Chakra

Personal Power: Associated with personal power and the ability to take charge of one's life and actions.

Self-Esteem: Governs self-esteem and the perception of one's own influence and impact.

Willpower and Motivation: Links to our inner drive and determination to pursue our goals and ambitions and persevere despite obstacles.

Transformation: Connects to transformation and the ability to overcome challenges, turning them into opportunities for growth.

Focus and Clear Thinking: Influences the ability to think clearly, make decisions, and make progress.

THE MINDSET SHIFT

To create lasting shifts toward improved behaviors, let's explore the mindsets that contribute to your pet's barking, jumping, nipping, or chewing and how they parallel similar motivations and themes in your life.

Mindset Shift with Unwanted Behaviors

Going from feeling frustrated and helpless when faced with your pet's unwanted behaviors *to* being proactive and confident in your abilities and training skills to encourage a confident, well-mannered pet.

Mindset Shift in Other Areas of Our Lives

Going From Limiting Mindsets Like >>

Suffering from indecision

Demanding perfectionism

Lacking esteem

Not believing in self and dreams

Relinquishing personal power by holding others' abilities in higher esteem

Lacking focus and follow-through

Postponing and distracting from getting started

Procrastinating through milestones such as "*I'll get to that when...*"

Feeling at the mercy of others

Unwilling to take creative risks

Showing up in limiting mindsets like:

I do not have the power to create the outcome of my own life.
I disempower myself to avoid accountability.
I do not give myself the credit or recognition I deserve.
Nothing I do is ever good enough.
I stagnate when trying to step into my power.

Going To Beneficial Mindsets Like >>

Harnessing your willpower
Living an empowered life
Taking action and completing missions
Being disciplined, dependable
Taking a creative approach to problem-solving
Overcoming obstacles and challenges strategically and confidently
Being inspired and joyful when approaching new projects
Taking accountability for your role in your pet's behavior
Making decisions and taking steps toward a bigger goal
Feeling comfortable in one's skin
Being confident, focused, and inspired
Having patience to stick with tasks through completion

Showing up in beneficial mindsets like:

I find joy and inspiration in putting creations out into the world.
I give myself recognition for my effort and accomplishments.
I have the knowledge, abilities, and drive to make a difference.
I am a problem solver committed to tackling complex tasks.
I am disciplined, focused, and committed to my pursuits.
I am comfortable in my own skin.

TRANSLATING YOUR PET'S BEHAVIOR

Let's explore some motivations and energetic themes that may be contributing to our pup's behavior stemming from the third chakra. Barking, jumping, nipping, and other unwanted behaviors signal an opportunity to revisit matters of empowerment, taking action, self-sabotage, and frustration.

> *Where are you disempowering yourself?*
> *What projects are you putting off?*
> *Where are you feeling stuck?*
> *Where can you let go of self-sabotage?*

Where are you disempowering yourself?
In managing unwanted pet behaviors, we often discover parallels in our own lives where we perceive others to be more capable and adept than us. When we compare ourselves to others, we can question our abilities and give up before even starting. By recognizing areas to empower ourselves and affirming our abilities, we create opportunities to take pride in what we've achieved. We trust that our efforts make a significant impact, both in our pet's behavior and in our own life. When we let go of the mindset that others have more influence or superior abilities and commit to valuing and growing our own skillset, we find a newfound sense of joy and inspiration.

Practical Insight: Reflect on your achievements and capabilities in pet training, relationships, and career. Give yourself the credit you deserve and acknowledge your skills. Surround yourself with supportive influences that encourage your power and abilities.

What projects are you putting off?
Unwanted pet behaviors can result from our pet drawing attention to our procrastination of a specific project or creative endeavor due to a lack of focus, a tendency for perfectionism, or fear of failure. We may fall into the habit of hopping from one creative idea to another without seeing any through to completion. We may get bogged down in the minutia of tasks because we lack clarity on the bigger project. When we hit a bump in the road or feel frustrated with the progress, we give up. Or perhaps we judge our own creations before they even take shape. These mindsets disempower us and create an internal struggle from the first to the final steps. Understand that progress is achieved through consistent effort, focus, and determination. Even small steps keep the momentum and can lead to new steps and more inspiration.

Practical Insight: To address procrastination, identify its root causes. If it's a lack of focus, create accountability for yourself by breaking your goals into manageable steps and setting deadlines. If perfectionism or fear of failure is the root cause, approach the project from a place of joy and creativity rather than judgment. Break down tasks into smaller, manageable steps and set deadlines to maintain focus. Remember that small, consistent efforts lead to significant progress.

Where are you feeling stuck?
When dealing with a pet's unwanted behavior, you may find that you feel stuck and frustrated, leading to stagnation. Similarly, these issues can creep into other areas of your life. Just as our animal companions benefit from moving around or using active commands like Touch to redirect pent-up energy that leads to barking, chewing, and jumping, when we face our own challenges or are working toward a goal, it's important to keep moving forward and avoid stagnation. Changing any habit requires at least 30 days of commited effort. During that period, we must be mindful, observant, and consistent about the thoughts we allow in, steps we take daily toward our creative vision, and carving

out time for activities that help fan the flame and creative spark. As we experience progress and find more flow in our decisions, we'll see a positive shift in our pet's behavior and our projects.

Practical Insight: Just as you need to be consistent with your pet's training, train yourself to find the momentum to take smaller steps. Challenge yourself to set clear goals and take actionable steps to achieve them. Find a partner—whether a journal, human, or animal companion—to help you stay accountable and disciplined and to remind you of your progress on days you don't feel inspired.

Where can you let go of self-sabotage?
Self-sabotage keeps us stagnant and breeds frustration, which is a very potent formula for a cycle of self-resentment and disappointment. Self-sabotage often shows up as procrastination. Although frustrating, sometimes it's less daunting to spend our time and energy focusing on trying to "fix" a situation rather than engaging in time spent working on our own projects. We keep ourselves overly busy, fluttering from task to task so that we don't have to focus on a big project at hand. And in these cycles, our pets bark, jump, and nip at us as a means to encourage us to focus. Self-sabotage can hinder progress, both in pet training and in personal growth. Perhaps we have the know-how to create something impactful but are not willing to risk criticism from others. Or maybe our own standard of perfection keeps us from moving forward with a project. We may avoid taking a first step or releasing anything into the world until it's flawless.

Practical Insight: Replace self-sabotage with inspired action and perseverance. Remind yourself that mistakes are part of the learning process and a natural aspect of improvement. When you face challenges, it's an opportunity for growth, not a reason for self-blame. This shift in perspective will benefit both you and your pet.

MANAGING UNWANTED BEHAVIORS TRAINING

Managing unwanted behaviors calls you to take responsibility for the role you play in your pet's life, and also in your own. If you are avoiding a calling, a task, or looking at a broader energetic pattern in your life, your animal companion may call you on it through disruptive patterns.

Behaviors you might not love—like barking, jumping, digging, chewing, and nipping—come naturally to dogs. However, they might not be appropriate within your pack. In those cases, ensure your pet is getting enough stimulation and leverage the principles of positive reinforcement to communicate to your dog what is acceptable and what is not.

Providing Sufficient Physical & Mental Exercise

To effectively manage unwanted behaviors, it's crucial to understand their root cause. Often, these behaviors arise from boredom or escalating frustration. Therefore, ensuring your pup receives ample physical exercise and mental stimulation is essential. Engaging interactive toys and practicing commands are valuable tools in keeping your pup's mind occupied. You may even consider enlisting a dog walker to take your furry friend on an adventure while you're away, which can help curb unwanted behaviors.

Interrupting Behaviors

To interrupt barking, you can create a moment of silence by clapping or using a squeaky toy to interrupt your pup gently. Once your pup stops barking, calmly acknowledge the silence with a "YES" and redirect their energy into more suitable activities using active commands. Providing appropriate toys or activities can help channel their excess energy constructively.

Managing Jumping

Jumping is another common behavior that can be managed effectively through consistent techniques. Refrain from giving your pup attention, eye contact, or engagement when they jump. Instead, cross your arms and turn away, ensuring they understand that jumping leads to losing your attention. Calmly and confidently praise and reward them only when all four paws are on the ground, encouraging more appropriate behavior.

Nipping

Pups explore the world through their mouths, and nipping is common, especially during teething. Provide appropriate teething items like bully sticks, teething rings, or chilled washcloths to soothe their discomfort. When they nip during play, respond with a sharp "ouch" to interrupt them, then briefly stop engaging with them and withdraw attention. When your pup has calmed down, offer a toy to redirect their behavior and praise them when they make better choices.

Chewing

Interrupt and redirect your pup, offering them a better outlet for their excess energy, like a toy or a walk for fresh air. Additionally, do desensitization work and safeguard valuable items and wires to prevent destructive chewing.

Remember, managing unwanted behaviors is about building trust and guiding your pup to make better choices. Consistency, understanding their motivations, and positive reinforcement are key to successful training. With patience and dedication, your pup will learn more constructive ways to interact with their environment and you.

Troubleshooting

Understanding the Basis for Barking. Barking can be of various types, including territorial, alert, anxious, defensive, attention, frustration, and play barking. To manage territorial, defensive, or anxious barking, focus on building your pup's confidence. Providing them with a safe space, such as a crate or a gated area, can be helpful. If the barking is frustration-based rooted in seeking attention, ignoring your furry friend until there is a moment of quiet is a better strategy. Always remember to funnel excess energy into a more productive pursuit.

Praising Good Choices. Consistent feedback and encouragement are vital during training. Always acknowledge and calmly praise your pup whenever they make good choices or display desirable behaviors. This positive reinforcement solidifies their understanding of what is acceptable. It's just as crucial to avoid reinforcing unwanted behaviors inadvertently. Refrain from making eye contact and turn away when your pup displays undesirable actions.

Consistency, Consistency, Consistency. Maintaining consistency is paramount for successful behavior management. Ensure that everyone in the household follows the same rules and guidelines during training. Avoid exceptions, as it may confuse your pup and hinder progress.

Desensitization. If your pup exhibits undesirable behaviors around specific triggers, like their leash coming out before a walk, desensitization can be helpful. Gradually expose them to these items in short spurts throughout the day, offering high-value treats when acting appropriately to create positive associations and help them remain calm and collected.

Additional Considerations

Frustration. When managing unwanted behaviors, it is common to feel frustrated. Remember that your pup is inviting you to step into your own power more fully, and that begins with reaffirming how you feel about these behaviors. Rather than associating and imbuing them with the energy of frustration and helplessness, reaffirm that you have the ability, skills, and determination to create a shift and visualize what you want to see take its place. That way, you are projecting to your furry friend the better choices you are asking for from a place of that energetic resonance rather than from a place of frustration and what is not working. As you try to redirect our pup, frustration can seep in, creating frenetic energy around the situation that your pets picks up on and matches. Modeling the calmer energy you want to see from your pet can be the strongest catalyst for change.

Putting Out Fires vs. Empowering Transformation. As pet parents, especially if we have multiple members in our pack, we often spend our time and energy putting out fires or focusing on the pet who isn't complying. We manage unwanted behaviors rather than proactively create change by empowering our loved ones and pets to transform.

Rather than being in the mindset of correcting or constantly putting out fires, we can focus our time and energy on rewarding those that are complying and setting up training, establishing protocols for success, and determining ways to properly connect so the entire pack feels more empowered. This means less time and energy goes toward managing issues, and more is spent creating joyful output, whether it's an artistic endeavor, a creative pursuit, or simply opportunities to spend more enjoyable time together.

Catastrophizing. Sometimes, despite all our training efforts and focus on our energetic connection, our pets have a "bad day." They consistently miss the wee wee pad, act out, are extra nippy, or have a particularly reactive moment during a walk.

It's easy to feel discouraged, frustrated, or like a failure in those instances. We catastrophize, extrapolating that this is how things are going to be from here on out. But sometimes, our pets have the equivalent of a grumpy day, emotional outburst, or panic attack. And this is normal.

Our pups go through moods just like us. This means we might have a perfect day with our pups followed by a very challenging one, making it easy to feel all training has been lost. These setbacks are temporary and will pass as long as we stay consistent with training. And just as important as it is to manage our energy during the challenging times, we want to make a point of celebrating the victories. We can't control everything, but we can empower ourselves by perceiving each moment as a clean slate.

CASE STUDIES

Case Study #1

An Alert to Stay on Track

Let's explore how our energy, mindsets, and actions affect our pet's behavior through the case study of a helpful Maltese, Belle. Belle's insistent barking invited her pet parent to drop her habit of procrastination and adopt a more empowered and focused stance not only with Belle's training but toward her career as well.

Amidst the persistent clamor of determined barks, I walked into a household where the simple act of making breakfast for Belle, a spirited Maltese, revealed underlying fears her pet parent held toward her writing career.

The pet parent, a remarkable New Yorker and celebrated author, had reached out for help in addressing Belle's relentless barks for attention. Under the chaos of preparing salmon and fresh greens for her pup, a far more complex dynamic began to emerge.

Belle's incessant barking was just the tip of the iceberg, calling attention to an overlooked obligation to herself. By the time the pet parent had prepared Belle's breakfast and cleaned up, her morning ritual was just getting started. As the pet parent detailed her and Belle's daily routine, she took clean plates out of the cabinet to give them a quick polish with a dish towel before putting them right back, then went about reshuffling and relocating items that already were organized and tidy. Throughout this process, I watched as Belle barked and jumped up at her pet parent's leg. I patiently observed, noticing we were well into our training session, but there wasn't much morning left.

It was obvious to me that the issue of Belle's barking was not centered around demanding service and attention from her pet parent, as I had initially presumed. Rather, it expressed Belle's frustration watching her pet parent spend time tidying up an already immaculate household.

I asked the pet parent how she would ideally spend her mornings if Belle's behavior was not creating a disruption. The way only a talented author could, her words beautifully brought to life mornings spent writing in her office with a piping hot cup of coffee, vanilla creamer wafting in the air, and moody music in the background. She explained that this was her morning routine for every book she ever wrote. In this space, her creativity would flow. But lately, Belle's behavior prevented her from engaging in her project. And wouldn't you know, the timing of Belle's barking coincided with her publisher green-lighting her next book.

This well-respected, brilliant, accomplished, and charismatic New Yorker was procrastinating. And serving Belle and tending to the home was a great excuse to stall.

When I gently brought this to her attention, there was a long sigh, and the pet parent finally took a seat at the table across from me. Belle's barking and attention-seeking behavior stopped, too, and she laid down sweetly by her pet parent's feet.

Belle's mom shared that every time she was faced with starting a new project, concerns that it might not live up to the success of her past endeavors would set in. She recognized this pattern and acknowledged procrastination was a common way she dealt with these fears of inadequacy. With that understanding, it was clear that the issue motivating Belle's barking was an alert to get going.

With that realization and some training tools and tips, Belle's mom was determined to face her procrastination head-on. I was pleased to receive an early text from her one morning. It was a photo of a steaming cup of coffee sitting next to a laptop, with the view of Belle snoozing on the couch in front of her.

Practical Insight: This case study illuminated a profound truth—we can be our own biggest roadblock. Belle's mom changed her habits and used time to focus on her career pursuits. Belle's barking served as a poignant reminder of the intricate interplay between our projects and the role our pets play in holding us accountable to ourselves. Here, Belle undertakes the role of calling out behavior that is keeping her pet parent from success and fulfillment in her career.

Case Study #2

The Flame Within Fritz

Whether in the form of excess energy for Fritz or the frenetic, unfocused energy of worry for his mom, understanding how to tame the inner fire was a path to benefit both.

When Fritz, an empathetic and sensitive pup, began exhibiting challenging behaviors, his pet parent turned to me for clarity through an animal communication session. Her concerns included Fritz's recent excessive barking, nipping, and engaging in mischievous outbursts that were increasingly hard to manage.

During our sessions with Fritz, he shared his emotional experience when things got intense at home. He explained his experience using the metaphor of an internal fire.

Whether it was the mailman delivering packages or the excitable activities of his furry pack members, he explained that he would feel a surging fire within, building up and creating an overwhelming sense of energy. In response, Fritz sought release by engaging in various behaviors–running, jumping, barking, and nipping his furry siblings– as a way to expel this pent-up intensity.

As I conveyed Fritz's description of a growing fire of frenetic energy within his belly, his pet parent confessed she knew exactly what that felt like. She, too, was battling her own internal fire. Interestingly, she was married to a fireman. When she worried about her husband's demanding profession, she turned to busying herself with various tasks and busy work for fear that if she sat or stopped in place, the worry of her husband's safety would consume her. Although she tried to manage her concerns by focusing on minutiae, the worries she harbored deep within still created unfocused and frenetic energy Fritz mirrored. The metaphorical fire that Fritz felt in his belly reflected the frenetic, fiery energy of worry that consumed his mom when her husband was on duty.

Fritz had a simple request, one that would serve as the key to managing this inner fire for both of them: more walks, especially along the water. Living blocks from the beach, his pet parent readily embraced this solution to help him expend that excess energy, soothe the fiery sensations within, and help her find more empowered and focused outlets for her feelings and worry. Through these walks, they were able to tame their fire within and refocus their energy on more productive outlets.

Practical Insight: Fritz's story reminds us that when we feel disempowered, it can manifest in various forms, be it the pent-up energy of an exuberant pup or the frenetic pace of our own lives. By embracing this understanding of how our pets reflect our energetic terrain, we can work toward refocusing our energy into more productive and beneficial habits, leading to a sense of balance, calm, and serenity that benefits us both.

Activities

CHASING NEW HABITS

Practice Mindful Activities. Engage in activities that naturally promote movement and mindfulness, such as yoga, guided meditation, or even simply spending time walking in nature. These activities can help you develop the habit of being more focused and inspired and build your momentum as you work toward bigger goals and projects.

STAY COMMAND TRAINING

The idea is to get your dog to STAY until you release him, allowing him to safely and temporarily stay put, whether to work on impulse control, engage in a fun game of hide-and-seek, or avoid a potentially dangerous situation.

1. Gesture for your dog to SIT without using the verbal cue.
2. Put your hand up, palm out (as if to motion stop) for 1-2 seconds, then bring both hands to your chest.
3. Count silently to three, maintaining your dog's focus, then release him from the command by saying YES. If your dog gets up to receive the treat, praise and give him the treat. If your dog doesn't get up after you say YES, take a step back, encouraging him to move to receive the treat.
4. If at any point your dog moves before you release him, start over by getting a silent SIT and try again.
5. Repeat this process, gradually increasing the number of seconds at a time that you are asking your dog to STAY until he is consistently performing the STAY command for 15 seconds. Only then should you add the verbal cue "STAY."
6. Challenge your dog by adding distance to the command. Gesture for your dog to SIT without using the verbal cue (hand gesture only). Give the verbal cue "STAY" paired with the hand gesture, and take two steps back, maintaining your dog's focus.
7. Count silently to three, maintaining your dog's focus, then release him from the command by saying YES. If your dog gets up to receive the treat, praise and give him the treat. If your dog doesn't get up after you say YES, take a step back, encouraging him to move to receive the treat.
8. If at any point your dog moves before you release him, start over by getting a silent SIT and try again.
9. Repeat this process 7-10 times, gradually increasing the distance between you and your dog when you ask him to STAY.

BUILDING THE STAY COMMAND

Wean out the treats first through delaying rewards and then via an intermittent schedule of reinforcement. Always reward better performances with higher-value treats. Try starting this command in the standing or lying down positions. If successful, your dog should not change positions during the STAY command.

Once your dog can perform the STAY command without distraction indoors, practice the command in different places with different distractions. Over time, you should gradually increase the distance between you and your dog. Remain in your dog's sight until she understands how to stay. Then, you can try leaving the room after giving the STAY command.

Once your dog has mastered the STAY command, try practicing with distractions. Get a friend to talk or squeak a toy. Your dog should not move at all despite the distraction. If you want to try this outside without a leash, always be sure you are in a fenced-in area.

GUEST REACTIVITY
& Putting Yourself First

OVERVIEW

Shared Motivation
Emotional Needs for Belonging and Love

Energetic Overlay
Fourth Chakra affecting Heart, Lungs

Universal Themes
Intimacy, Compassion, Devotion, Trust, Vulnerability,
Courage, Loyalty, & Self-Acceptance

Translating Your Pet's Behavior
Where can you be more mindful about who and what enters your space?
Where are you trying to anticipate and manage everyone else's emotions?
Where can you be more loyal to yourself and those who intimately matter?
Where can you be open to receiving more love, compassion, and acceptance from yourself and others?

Guest Reactivity

When our energetic boundaries are not properly implemented or respected, our animal companions may pick up on it and interpret people entering our space as threatening. Guest desensitization helps build trust and lets our pets know that when others are invited into our space, it is safe. Through this process, our furry friends learn how to create a positive association with visitors, the proper protocol when they arrive, and how to start with small steps and then work up to the excitement of guests entering your home. As you translate your pet's behavior, explore matters of intimacy, compassion, loyalty, self-love, and emotional boundaries—all themes related to the fourth chakra and guest reactivity.

What Is Guest Reactivity?

Guest reactivity is when a pet, often a dog, reacts with anxiety, fear, or overenthusiasm upon encountering visitors in the home. This reaction can range from timidly hiding to barking, jumping, or being excessively excited to growling, lunging, or even nipping. Effective training and desensitization techniques encourage pets to be more comfortable and better behaved during these social interactions, promoting a more welcoming and comfortable atmosphere for both our animal companions and guests.

UNDERSTANDING MOTIVATION

If your pet displays guest reactivity by reacting nervously or aggressively to visitors—or either you or your pet are experiencing physical symptoms with your heart or lungs—it's an opportunity to delve into matters of trust, intimacy, compassion, passion, vulnerability, and self-acceptance. Consider how these emotions may influence your pet's behavior and how they relate to your own feelings regarding their reactions to guests.

Parallel in Maslow's Pyramid: Belonging and Love Needs

According to Maslow's theory, our need for love and belonging are high-ranking. We all desire trusting, intimate, and compassionate relationships. Much like humans, pets also seek to form meaningful connections and bonds with those around them. When they react defensively, guest reactivity in pets can be seen as a response to feeling vulnerable and a reflection of our need to be more mindful of how we are getting our own love and belonging needs met.

Parallel in the Chakra System: Fourth Chakra

Being kind, practicing forgiveness, and cultivating a grateful attitude can help bring the fourth chakra into alignment. This is crucial for fostering love and compassion and building harmonious relationships with others, which leads to a more intimate connection with oneself and the world.

Signs It's In Balance

- Experiencing deep and unconditional love for oneself and others.
- Feeling a sense of empathy and compassion toward all living beings.
- Forming healthy and meaningful relationships based on trust and openness.
- Having a stable emotional state, neither suppressing nor overwhelming emotions.

Signs It's Out of Balance

- Struggling with a sense of feeling isolated, lonely, or bitter.
- Demonstrating jealousy or possessiveness in relationships.
- Experiencing difficulties in forgiving oneself or others.
- Suffering from heart-related health issues or respiratory problems.

Unique Themes Attributed to Fourth Chakra

Love and Belonging: Closely associated with the capacity to love unconditionally and fosters belonging for oneself and others.

Healing and Compassion: Center for emotional healing and plays a vital role in the process through compassion, both for ourselves and others.

Intimacy: Fosters a sense of deep trust and connection with all living beings and the world, promoting a feeling of unity and oneness.

Stability and Integration: Bridges the physical and spiritual realms, encouraging balance and integration of the lower and higher aspects of our being.

Loyalty: Linked to the practice of loving devotion.

THE MINDSET SHIFT

Understanding and facing these underlying emotions and mindsets help your pet build healthier, more positive relationships with guests and create an environment where they feel a stronger sense of belonging and love in their interactions with others.

Mindset Shift with Guest Reactivity

Going from feeling overwhelmed, anxious, and unsure when your pet encounters visitors *to* feeling confident and optimistic that you can create a compassionate and trusting atmosphere for both your pet and your visitors.

Mindset Shift in Other Areas of Our Lives

Going From Limiting Mindsets Like >>

Perceiving others entering your space as a threat
Not trusting others to respect your emotional boundaries
Having a bleeding heart
Having conditional self-love and acceptance
Hiding true emotions and vulnerability
Projecting an idealized, sanitized image of self to impress others
Idealizing relationships
Being emotionally explosive or indulgent
Displaying toxic positivity
Being overly attached or noncommittal
Being indiscriminately loyal
Seeking acceptance and belonging
Being emotionally shut off

Showing up in limiting mindsets like:

I do not trust myself to set up healthy boundaries around my heart and my energy.
I do not deserve to be treated with the same compassion I show others.
I do not trust that people will stay if they see my vulnerability.
I would be left alone if others knew my true emotions and feelings.
I am not worthy of love if I feel anger and resentment.

Going To Beneficial Mindsets Like >>
Being forgiving and compassionate
Showing appreciation and gratitude to others
Being open-hearted and emotionally available
Being playful and innocent
Captivating hearts and admiration
Being discerning and selective with intimate relationships
Firmly and gracefully holding your boundaries
Following your heart
Being loyal to the right people
Remaining hopeful
Being courageous

Showing up in beneficial mindsets like:

I prioritize the most important relationships in my life, including the one with myself.
I am worthy of love and compassion, and I embrace the kindness I extend to others.
I trust my connections to deepen when I allow myself to be vulnerable.
I surround myself with those who value my true emotions and feelings.
I attract supportive and understanding relationships by sharing my genuine thoughts and feelings.
My worthiness of love is not conditional.

TRANSLATING YOUR PET'S BEHAVIOR

Guest Reactivity signals an opportunity to revisit themes around the fourth chakra. Let's explore some of these major themes, including self-care, compassion, empathy, and intimacy, and how they show up in various areas of our lives.

> *Where can you be more mindful about who and what enters your space?*
>
> *Where are you trying to anticipate and manage everyone else's emotions?*
>
> *Where can you be more loyal to yourself and those who intimately matter?*
>
> *Where can you be open to receiving more love, compassion, and acceptance from yourself and others?*

Where can you be more mindful about who and what enters your space?

Just as we would not leave the door to our apartment or home unlocked for anyone to enter freely, we must be mindful of our energetic boundaries. Our surroundings can harbor more than just physical objects; they hold memories, emotions, and the energy of past occupants. If we are not mindful, energetic debris can linger long after their physical presence leaves. Being discerning about what we allow to enter or remain in our life, heart, or home is crucial to fostering a nurturing space for both us and our pets. When we are not discriminating with our emotional and energetic boundaries, our pets' reaction to those entering our hearts and homes may reflect it.

Practical Insight: Whether news broadcasts, emotions, or people, be careful about who or what you allow to enter your and your pet's energetic space. Understand that your animal companion also experiences the energy of that which you welcome into your life. If planning a gathering, compassionately prepare your pet by explaining what is about to happen before your guests arrive.

Where are you trying to anticipate and manage everyone else's emotions?
As sensitive pet parents, some of us have a tendency to subconsciously take on others' emotional baggage or assume responsibility for their experiences, reactions, and emotions. We expend a lot of energy trying to manage and protect everyone's feelings. This plays out with visitors entering our space and extends to our dynamics with friends, family, and in our career. Just as we should trust our guests to manage their interactions and emotions themselves to avoid unnecessary stress for ourselves, we should release the need to anticipate and manage everyone else's feelings in other areas of our lives. When we shift our focus to maintaining our own emotional equilibrium instead, we create an environment that is more supportive of our pet's emotional needs.

Practical Insight: With guest reactivity, even the thought that your guest might take your pet's standoffishness personally may create stress for you, which your pet picks up on. Trust that your guests can handle their feelings and reactions, and preemptively address your pet's preferences and boundaries with guests, explaining, "My cat needs a little time to warm up," or "My dog doesn't like to be petted on the head."

Where can you be more loyal to yourself and those who intimately matter?
Our pets teach us valuable lessons in prioritizing loyalty to the right relationships. However, even with the best intentions, we sometimes

inadvertently de-prioritize ourselves or those closest to us, such as prioritizing a visitor's feelings over our pet's during guest desensitization training. Much like the unwavering devotion we receive from our pets, loyalty in human relationships is rooted in consistent care, support, and dedication. This extends to being loyal to ourselves—an aspect often overlooked in our earnest efforts to nurture others. Practicing self-care includes treating ourselves with the same kindness and compassion we extend to those dearest to us, making ourselves a priority, and being discerning about with whom we share our intimate thoughts and emotions.

Practical Insight: Carefully evaluate your relationships, prioritizing yourself and those who contribute positively to your life. Reflect on instances where you have not operated from a place of self-love, self-preservation, and compassion, and how themes around loyalty and self-care are applicable not only with your pet but also with family members, friends, and even your job, boss, and co-workers.

Where can you be open to receiving more love, compassion, and acceptance from yourself and others?

We all have the desire to feel profoundly loved, accepted, and significant. Some of us find it difficult to remain open-hearted to love and acceptance because it has been conditional, painful, or unrequited in the past. For many of us, the only time we feel truly safe receiving love is from pets, but it's essential to be open to receiving love, compassion, and acceptance from ourselves and others as well. Our animal companions are here to bring more love into our lives and teach us how to truly accept ourselves. Only then can we lead with open hearts, let others in, and share intimately honest and heartfelt moments like those we share with our pets with others.

Practical Insight: Practice self-care and self-compassion, with a focus on treating yourself with kindness and respect. Even if it makes you feel vulnerable or uncomfortable, allow others to do the same. Live in the present, forgive yourself for past experiences, and be fully open to who you are today without judgment.

GUEST DESENSITIZATION TRAINING

When guests come over, it's crucial to be emotionally present with your pup and attend to their needs in the moment. Equally important is ensuring your guests' safety and comfort by preventing your pup from jumping or nipping for attention. As you approach guest desensitization training, remember to bring compassionate energy into interactions with your pet, those you invite to enter your space, and yourself.

Safety First

Use physical barriers like baby gates to distance your pup from the door and ensure the visitor's safety. Be aware of the signals you send to your pup and create a safe space for them during the visit. Engage your pup in activities or commands to keep them occupied and connected with you.

Classic Desensitization

Address the behavior using traditional training techniques, starting from the earliest signs of stress and gradually working your way up to a visitor arriving. Break the process into manageable steps for your pup to create a positive association with guests arriving. For example, start practicing commands in view of the door with your pet safely behind a doggy gate, then on leash in the same room as the front door, and eventually untethered near the door. The following exercises will guide you through some helpful steps preparing for guest arrivals.

Doorbell Desensitization

- During playtime (away from your door), play a recording of your doorbell, ring the doorbell yourself, or have a family member ring the doorbell.
- If your pup ignores the doorbell, mark the silence with a YES, praise, and reward.
- If your pup reacts to the doorbell, calmly redirect his attention with an active command like Touch, mark silence with a YES, praise, and reward for paying attention to you. If you become stressed, your pup will sense a change in your behavior and assume there is a problem.
- Repeat this in sessions of 1-2 times, 3-5 times throughout the day, for a couple of weeks.

Giving Your Pup a Job

- Ring the doorbell or have someone ring the doorbell for you.
- When your dog approaches the door, toss a treat on a doggy bed and tell your pup, "Place" or "Go to Bed."
- Repeat this throughout the day, in short spurts, until your pup reliably goes to her bed to earn a treat when you approach the door.

Desensitization to the Door Opening

- Once your pup reliably goes to his bed when you approach the door, begin slowly opening the door while he is relaxing on the doggy bed. If your dog has a strong STAY command, ask your pup to STAY.
- If your pup remains on his bed while you open the door, mark it with a YES, praise, and treat. If your pup tries to get up, use a warning sound like "no thank you" or "aaaht," close the door immediately, and try again slower.

- Repeat this throughout the day, in short spurts, until your pup reliably stays on his bed while you open the door. Once that is achieved, increase the difficulty by ringing the doorbell while your dog is on his bed. Mark with a YES, praise, and treat if your dog stays on his bed.

Adding the Element of a Visitor

- Have a friend/neighbor/doorman come up and ring the bell. Instruct your pet to go to their "Place" or bed. Open the door without having your guest come in. Instruct your visitor to ignore your pup and avoid eye contact.
- If your pup remains calm, mark the silence with a calm YES, praise, and treat. Calmly verbally thank your pup as she remains calm. Mark 5, 7, and then 10 seconds of silence with a YES and toss a treat as she remains quiet and obedient.
- Once your pup remains calm at the sight of a visitor, invite your visitor a couple of steps into the apartment. As the visitor enters the threshold, have them drop a high-value treat for your pup.
- Repeat this in sessions of 3-5 times, as often as possible throughout the day, for a couple of weeks.
- As your pup becomes more comfortable, you can practice having your visitor enter and take a seat away from the door.

Respecting Physical Boundaries

Not all pups enjoy physical contact, so we want to be mindful of their comfort levels. Respect your pup's personal boundaries and teach others to do the same. This includes asking your guests to refrain from petting them or speaking to your pet in excited tones. Uphold your pup's boundaries outside the home, like during walks, to build trust.

Allowing for Space

Always provide a space for your pup to retreat to and ask guests to respect their comfort level. Allow your pup to approach guests at his or her own pace and intervene if necessary. Be mindful of your pup's sensitivities, such as loud noises, and give constant feedback to maintain a positive environment.

Troubleshooting

- Always try to greet guests and each other away from the front door, as that tends to become a very energetically charged place.
- Practice knocking on the door and eventually opening it, pretending to welcome guests in as dress rehearsals. Use Looks and Touches to get them to an appropriate area away from the door where they can be rewarded. Eventually, the goal is that they will run directly to that space any time they hear the door knock or doorbell ring, waiting for the treat rather than rushing toward the door.
- A rapid series of easy commands can also be a great way to refocus pups if they are overly excited and enthusiastic.
- Energy is everything, so make sure you are grounded and in the moment with the pups. Verbally, less can be more when in stressful or exciting situations.

Additional Considerations

Respecting Emotional Boundaries. Healthy emotional boundaries include modeling them for our pup and not allowing anyone to come into our home and treat us in a disrespectful manner. We model clear emotional boundaries through the example we set. If we do not, our pup may pick up on the energetic exchange and perceive this person as harmful, ill-intentioned, or a threat and generalize that perception to anyone entering the home. On the flip side, are we the ones who need to better respect others' emotional boundaries? Are we getting overly familiar, personal, or friendly without permission? As we revisit our interactions and boundaries around guests, it is an opportunity to revisit how we interact with others who may be more emotionally and energetically reserved.

Courage. Our pets display courage when they face new experiences or meet unfamiliar people, encouraging us to do the same. By confronting challenges with courage, we set a powerful example for our pets and empower them to face new experiences and people with open hearts and minds.

If our pups seem nervous, upset, anxious, or act out, remember that they are working through their own perceptions of what it means to be vulnerable with a new person in the home. We can lovingly nurture and reassure our animal companions while still helping them make better choices and learn to be independent. Through this process, they learn to trust us with their emotional reactions and learn positive ways to communicate that they are uncomfortable and need help changing their perception of a situation. In turn, this allows them to have more courage in other aspects of their training.

Guest Positive. When working on guest desensitization with your furry friend, you also want to consider whether your pet is mirroring true feelings you might be experiencing. How do you honestly perceive guests? Do you also share your pet's uneasy feelings about a particular person? You may be social or love to entertain, but is there any part of hosting that taps into a tendency to overgive or people-please? Do friends constantly come over and dump their emotional baggage on you? Does your partner have a friend you don't like having in your home? Is hosting extended family dinners an obligation you find triggering? Are you weary of inviting over someone new you've been dating because you've been hurt before in relationships?

Empathic Tendencies. Pet parents often notice that when their animal companion is around certain people, their behavior changes, either becoming more calm, compliant, or playful or perhaps more fearful, difficult, or reactive. If you are an empath or a sensitive person, you know what it feels like when someone else's energy enters your field or you take on their emotions. Our animal companions, especially the sensitive ones, pick up on those same energies and emotions of the people around them. This can be confusing to them, as they may not always realize that the emotions they are sensing are not theirs. If the feelings they are taking on are fear-based, like anger, insecurity, or sadness, our pets may not know what to do with those confusing emotions. It can cause them to be anxious or reactive—displaying behaviors like jumping, chewing, digging, and barking—or they may absorb those emotions in an effort to heal others, sometimes resulting in behavioral or health problems. Being mindful about what and who we allow into our space manages what energy and emotions your pet is exposed to.

Vulnerability & Intimacy. Next to a spouse, an animal companion may be our most intimate, honest relationship. Our animal companions see us when we are at our most vulnerable and can pick up on even subtle signals and shifts in our energy. Our furry companions show us their most authentic selves and act as a safe space for us to do the same. This intimacy is not shared with the world; it is an exclusive privilege. Our animal companions remind us that genuine, emotional intimacy is something precious to be earned through time, trust, and shared experiences.

Trust. Building trust with our pets during training, just as with human relationships, starts with vulnerability. They teach us the power of vulnerability and opening up to trusted friends and loved ones, sharing our thoughts and feelings. Trusting others with our emotions and experiences can deepen connections and lead to a more harmonious life, but sometimes, we lack the courage to do so.

CASE STUDIES

Case Study #1

Dudley's Tale of Transformation

Many expecting or new parents contact me for advice on how best to prepare their furry companion for a new baby. Their concerns often revolve around not being able to give everyone in the family the attention they want or are used to. One such story stands out. Let's dig into how one pet parent's willingness to be vulnerable led to a heartwarming tale of transformation.

I received a training inquiry from a mother who had recently welcomed a new baby into the family. But this was not the only change affecting the household. This pet parent had recently gotten remarried and everyone was still adjusting to the new blended family.

With a new husband and the demands of nurturing a newborn, the mother was concerned her teenage daughter from her previous marriage would not receive enough attention amidst the arrival of a stepfather and a new baby. Her concern also extended to Dudley, the family's beloved Yorkie.

Though this pet parent cherished every member of her family with unwavering love, she expressed a concern that had been on her heart and mind: with all the recent changes to her pack, she quipped that even a single fly entering their home might tip the balance.

Although her words were in jest, Dudley took the energy behind the message seriously, which translated to one of the most intense cases of guest reactivity I had ever encountered. He fiercely sought to protect his pet parent's boundaries, following the unintentional directive of not allowing anything or anyone else into the home. No one could get close to his pet parent without Dudley aggressively barking and trying to nip them.

As Dudley's guest reactivity escalated, it became a pressing concern for the family. Whether longtime friends or strangers, visitors were met with a protective, hyper-vigilant Yorkie. As a result, the chaos that ensued during these episodes exacerbated the pet parent's anxiety around guests. Her heart was torn between wanting to nurture her baby, create a harmonious blended family, reassure Dudley that he was still a cherished member of the pack, and make her visitors feel safe and welcomed.

One day, as she sat on the porch with her partner, the weight of the situation overwhelmed her. Tears welled up in her eyes, and she began to share her deepest fears. She admitted to her partner that she was struggling to balance her time and energy between her teenage daughter, the new baby, and Dudley. She confessed to feeling like she couldn't meet all their needs and was overwhelmed by a sense of inadequacy.

Her partner, attentive and understanding, listened with an open heart. Instead of offering quick solutions, he recognized the importance of acknowledging her vulnerability and feelings. Together, they decided to reevaluate their family dynamics and find ways to ensure that every member of the pack felt loved and included while also establishing times in the week for the new mother to get time for herself.

In the weeks that followed, the couple implemented a new approach. They created a shared schedule that allowed each family member, furry or not, to have dedicated bonding time with the pet parent. They reassured Dudley that he was still a vital part of the family and provided him with guest desensitization training to address his reactivity. As the family embraced these changes, Dudley felt more reassured and, through desensitization and the use of calming chews, he slowly became more open to visitors.

Practical Insight: Dudley's story teaches us the transformative power of open, vulnerable communication within our families. Sharing our fears, insecurities, and concerns creates an opportunity for understanding and collaboration. Sometimes, it's the acknowledgment of our limitations that opens the door to finding new ways to meet our needs and the needs of our loved ones. In Dudley's case, the family's compassion and willingness to adjust their dynamics so that every pack member's needs were met—including the new mom's—made him feel secure, ultimately leading to a more balanced and harmonious home.

Case Study #2
A Pivotal Desk Turn for Peaceful Homecomings

While many pet parents are aware of how furniture placement affects the aesthetic and flow of a home, this case highlights the profound impact of spatial arrangement in addressing specific pet behavior. This story reveals how even the orientation of a desk factors into how our pets perceive our preparedness to receive visitors to the home.

A call for help came from a woman whose home was being disrupted by her anxious pup's loud barking and protectiveness any time a mail or delivery person approached the home. Given that the pet parent ran a shipping business out of her home, this was a regular occurrence. The large golden retriever had assumed the role of an overzealous guard, perched at the window, ready to ward off any potential intruders, and she wasn't sure how to shift this behavior.

For this pet parent, her world revolved around her budding business, and her desk was her command center. Positioned catty-corner from the front door, facing a window that looked onto the serene backyard, she enjoyed brief breaks gazing outside as she diligently toiled at her desk. Unfortunately, this position left her back turned to the main entrance of the house, creating a blind spot for her and inadvertently causing distress to her vigilant pup.

When we began our session, it became evident that the pet parent's back to the door was a trigger for her dog's anxious behavior. To address this, we decided to make a pivotal change. Her desk was reoriented, facing the front door instead of the window, and a cozy dog bed was placed next to her workstation. The dog bed became an inviting sanctuary where her furry companion could lounge comfortably while still feeling connected to her and the activity surrounding the home.

The transformation was remarkable. The simple act of turning her desk signaled to her pup that she was in control of the space. The newfound layout conveyed to her pup a sense of trust, reassuring him she was fully aware of any approaching visitors. With that change in place, we then worked together to establish a protocol that involved the dog retreating to his bed any time someone approached the house.

The change was palpable, and it resonated with her pup. The once chaotic experience of delivery people approaching the home was now a non-event, and the stress in the home was replaced with calm and serenity. Her business endeavors continued, but they unfolded in the harmonious presence of her loyal companion, sharing the workspace without worry or disturbance.

Practical Insight: This case study serves as a reminder that our pets are highly sensitive to our environment and how alert they perceive us to be about new people entering our space. Simple changes can transform an anxious atmosphere into a harmonious and welcoming space, benefitting both the pet parent and the furry companion.

Activities

FALL IN LOVE WITH NEW HABITS

Unplug from Technology. Disconnect from digital devices regularly, especially during quality time with your pet. This conscious choice allows you to create a tech-free space for deepening your connection and presence with your furry friend.

Mindful Relationships. Extend the practice of being grounded and present to your relationships with others. Whether with friends, family, or colleagues, practice active listening and being fully present during interactions.

Gratitude Routines. Creating small morning routines where we nourish ourselves and our pets is a wonderful way to infuse self-care into our day. Morning coffee is a great time to practice a few commands with a furry friend and identify three things you are grateful for or excited about.

ENCHANTÉ COMMAND TRAINING

The French word for "nice to meet you" is Enchanté [on-shon-tay]. The idea is to get your dog to shake on cue, making it the perfect command to show off your pup's manners upon making a new acquaintance. Having the new person treat him as a reward is a great way for your dog to create a positive association with an unfamiliar face.

1. Kneel in front of your dog and have him SIT facing you, with a couple of feet between you two.
2. Extend your right hand toward your dog's right paw, palm up, just below his knee.
3. Mark the instant your dog places his paw in your hand with a YES, praise, and treat.
4. If your dog does nothing, gently tap the back of his paw with your ring finger and lift it into your hand, mark it with a YES, then release, praise, and treat.
5. Repeat this 7-10 times until your dog consistently places his paw in your hand for the treat.
6. Once your dog consistently shakes your hand 7-10 times in a row, add the verbal cue "ENCHANTÉ." Continue to mark the instant your dog shakes your hand with a YES, praise, and treat.

BUILDING THE ENCHANTÉ COMMAND

Wean out the treats first through delaying rewards and then via an intermittent schedule of reinforcement. Always reward better performances with higher-value treats or jackpots.

Mark natural Shakes when you see them with a YES, "Good Enchanté," and treat.

BENEVOLENT LEADERSHIP
& Speaking Your Truth

OVERVIEW

Shared Motivation
Esteem Needs for Prestige and Respect from Others

Energetic Overlay
Fifth Chakra affecting Thyroid, Throat, Neck, Ears, Mouth, Teeth

Universal Themes
Communication, Authenticity, Truth, Assertiveness, Leadership,
Being Heard, Empathy, Anger & Self-Criticism

Translating Your Pet's Behavior
In what situations or relationships do you feel unheard or silenced?
Where are you not speaking your truth?
Where are your actions not matching your words?
Where are you avoiding or relinquishing a leadership role?
Where can you let go of negative self-talk?
Where would it benefit you to verbalize your anger?

Benevolent Leadership

Learn how to leverage positive reinforcement and our energy to clearly, effectively, and authentically communicate the rules of the pack to our pets. Learn about the energy of a leader in nature and the dos and don'ts to ensure our pup feels cared for and content. As we translate our pet's behaviors, explore being authentic, finding our voice, standing in our truth, and feeling heard—all themes associated with benevolent leadership and the fifth chakra.

What Is Benevolent Leadership?

Rooted in collaboration and communication, benevolent leadership is an essential tool to create a positive, stress-free, and empathic pack dynamic. This approach involves true partnership, including open and clear communication through training and cues, as well as observing and actively listening to our pets' needs. By responding and creating an environment of cooperation with our animal companions, we build mutual trust and respect and strengthen the bond between pet and guardian.

UNDERSTANDING MOTIVATION

When you need to establish benevolent leadership—or you or your pet are experiencing symptoms around your thyroid, throat, neck, ears, mouth, teeth, or vocal cords—it is an opportunity to explore matters related to the fifth chakra. These include the power of your voice, communication, authenticity, truth, leadership, being heard, and overcoming negative self-talk. Consider how these elements play a role in your interactions with your pet and how they contribute to the dynamics of your relationship.

Parallel in Maslow's Pyramid: Esteem Needs for Prestige and Respect from Others

Maslow's Hierarchy of Needs factors in how esteem needs are met when we are held by others in prestige and respect. Providing benevolent leadership for our pets not only addresses our desire for respect but also allows our pets to feel valued when being enlisted to perform tasks alongside us and follow our commands. Prestige and respect, whether in the pet or human world, are earned through assertive guidance, authority, and authentic communication.

Parallel in the Chakra System: Fifth Chakra

Balancing the fifth chakra promotes effective communication. Engaging in practices like journaling, speaking affirmations, and engaging in honest self-reflection can help bring the fifth chakra into alignment. As a result, we express ourselves with confidence and experience more honest, authentic interactions with ourselves and others.

Signs It's In Balance
- Expressing oneself clearly and confidently without fear of judgment.
- Communicating with honesty and integrity.
- Listening actively and being able to empathize with others.
- Being comfortable with silence and knowing when to speak or stay quiet.

Signs It's Out of Balance
- Struggling to express thoughts or emotions openly and honestly.
- Experiencing difficulty in speaking up for oneself or setting boundaries.
- Engaging in gossip or talking excessively without meaningful communication.
- Suffering from frequent bouts of sore throat, ear aches, hoarseness, oral care issues, or thyroid imbalances.

Unique Themes Attributed to Fifth Chakra

Expression and Variety: Enables us to share our unique ideas, talents, and range of experiences with the world.

Communication and Authenticity: Governs effective communication, allowing us to speak our truth with conviction and clarity.

Listening and Empathy: Emphasizes the importance of approaching our interactions with others with empathy, including a balance between speaking and listening.

Voice and Power: Finding and using our authentic voice, empowering us to assert ourselves and make a positive impact through communication.

Healing and Purification: Using the power of words and communication as a tool for emotional release and purification.

THE MINDSET SHIFT

Negative mindsets and self-talk impact the authenticity and clarity of your communication and may hinder your ability to provide benevolent leadership. Affirming beneficial mindsets empowers you to lead with confidence and authenticity, helping both you and your pet build a stronger, more fulfilling connection.

Mindset Shift with Benevolent Leadership

Going from feeling that your pet doesn't listen to you because you don't carry the energy of a leader *to* embracing the role of a collaborative leader through two-way communication and positive feedback that strengthens the respect and bond with your furry friend.

Mindset Shift in Other Areas of Our Lives:

Going From Limiting Mindsets Like >>
Feeling restless
Operating from anger
Being uncommunicative, silent, or monotone
Being overbearing, bossy, or dominating
Being inauthentic or sarcastic
Being passive aggressive
Being dismissive or self-pitying
Being unreliable
Being self-righteous or militant
Being intolerant or accusatory
Being verbose
Being supplicant

Showing up in limiting mindsets like:

I am unable to verbalize my truth without hurting or disappointing others.
I am not worthy of standing in my own beliefs & principles.
I am unable to speak up for myself or my beliefs.
I am never heard when I speak my truth.
If I speak in anger, that will define me.

Going To Beneficial Mindsets Like >>
Being experiential, sensorial, or sensitive
Remaining empathic
Operating from personal freedom
Being curious and expressive
Being vivacious
Remaining communicative, sincere, and honest
Being direct and assertive
Being convincing
Being charismatic and engaging
Being collaborative
Being a problem solver
Being inclusive
Being authoritative
Being an advocate

Showing up in beneficial mindsets like:

I can express my truth with kindness and consideration while still standing my ground.
I have a unique perspective that deserves to be respected and valued.
I embrace my voice and advocate for what I believe in with conviction.
When I speak my truth, I am heard and understood by those who value me.
I learn and grow with each communication.

TRANSLATING YOUR PET'S BEHAVIOR

Our pets requiring stronger or more consistent benevolent leadership signals an opportunity to revisit themes around the fifth chakra, including matters dealing with finding our voice, being heard, standing in our truth, and communicating authentically. Let's dig into how these themes affect our leadership roles when it comes to our pets and other aspects of our lives.

> *In what situations or relationships do you feel unheard or silenced?*
> *Where are you not speaking your truth?*
> *Where are your actions not matching your words?*
> *Where are you avoiding or relinquishing a leadership role?*
> *Where can you let go of negative self-talk?*
> *Where would it benefit you to verbalize your anger?*

In what situations or relationships do you feel unheard or silenced? Sometimes, we believe we are not worthy of being heard or that our voice doesn't matter. We may feel our role is not to speak but merely mimic or repeat others. Or perhaps we attempt to speak, but our experiences are invalidated or our words are not acknowledged. In these scenarios, we tend to overexplain, bargain, or stop communicating altogether. As we learn how to best communicate, we develop our own distinctive "Voice" rooted in a style that feels natural and authentic to each of us. In doing so, our communication becomes more commanding, powerful, and effective.

Practical Insight: When in this mindset of not feeling heard or silenced, understand that your words have value and your opinions matter, and strive to be bolder in your expression, even if it feels uncomfortable at first. Identify the areas where you feel silenced or not heard to improve communication. Capture your thoughts and feelings on paper, then read them aloud. Mindfully observe how your words and voice sound filling the space and the energy they convey.

Where are you not speaking your truth?

Authentic communication is fundamental when interacting with both pets and people, especially in a leadership role. Some of us are more comfortable than others when speaking and communicating our thoughts, ideas, beliefs, and opinions. This may be due to concerns about hurting others or not feeling authoritative. If your words don't feel authentic once you speak them, they may have been passed down culturally or generationally rather than being your own truth or convictions. Embracing opportunities to be more direct, expressive, and unapologetically yourself allows you to communicate honestly and enhance your leadership skills.

Practical Insight: It's important to speak your truth authentically. Evaluate the situations in your life where you're not speaking your truth, standing up for yourself, or may be censoring your words or biting your tongue. Begin cultivating your voice and messages around truths that matter most to you. You can speak up not only on your behalf but for those who cannot speak for themselves, like the animals.

Where are your actions not matching your words?

Employing training methods that feel starkly incongruent with our natural tendencies is a common source of failure in communication for pet parents and their furry friends. When our pets perceive a misalignment between actions, words, and energy, it registers as inconsistency and inauthenticity. As a result, our animal companions feel the need to assume the leadership role in the pack, offering a semblance of security and hierarchy. The same way incongruencies between our words and actions affect our communication with pets, it can affect the way we communicate with others. If we are not walking our talk or mimicking someone else's style, our message will be muddled. Our credibility is compromised when there's an inconsistency in what our energy, words, and actions signal. Being mindful of aligning our words and actions builds trust and clarity in our relationships.

Practical Insight: Reflect on the areas in your life where your words do not match your actions. Focus on clarity and reliability in your interactions to strengthen your relationships and build credibility. Examine whether there are discrepancies in how you communicate your intentions. In pet training, seek out training methods that align with your true self, tendencies, and authentic leadership style.

Where are you avoiding or relinquishing a leadership role?
Undertaking leadership is important in our relationship with our pets, but also in broader aspects of our lives. Whether asserting yourself at work, in your relationships, or with your pet, stepping into a leadership role may seem daunting. We may be convinced that not having all the answers opens us up to being wrong, and we feel our role as a leader is fraudulent. We may hesitate to lead due to concerns about letting others down or fear of being seen as bossy. By addressing these hang-ups, we can lead more confidently in various areas of our lives.

Practical Insight: Ask yourself where you may be avoiding or relinquishing leadership and what concerns are keeping you from stepping into that role. Embrace the opportunity to lead and make decisions with self-assuredness, starting in areas you feel most confident.

Where can you let go of self-criticism?
The same way we would not speak harshly to our pets, we should avoid doing so to ourselves. Negative self-talk can permeate various aspects

of life, impacting confidence, communication, and even relationships, including those with our pets. These internal dialogues, often undermining and self-deprecating, create a mental environment that hinders personal growth. When we engage in habitual self-criticism, it not only affects our self-esteem but makes others less confident in our capabilities to be a positive influence in their life.

Practical Insight: Challenge and replace negative self-talk with positive affirmations. Be mindful of opportunities to encourage your pet with positive feedback, too. Making a habit of verbalizing positive perceptions of yourself and those around you can boost your self-esteem, self-confidence, and overall impression of yourself as a leader.

Where would it benefit you to verbalize your anger?

Just as it is instinctual for our pets to be reactive in certain situations, we also get triggered. Anger is a natural emotion that should not be suppressed. It's important to identify the situations in our lives where verbalizing anger can be beneficial. This doesn't mean lashing out but rather expressing our feelings constructively. Anger can be a powerful catalyst leading us to finally verbalize longstanding issues lingering beneath the surface. When done in a productive way, anger can convey that something is important to us, which can lead to newfound empathy and open lines of communication to express and understand how our actions affect each other.

Practical Insight: In difficult situations, openly communicate your feelings and needs while also being open to hearing the voice of others. Recognize that anger is a natural emotion; when expressed with empathy, it can lead to resolution.

BENEVOLENT LEADERSHIP TRAINING

As we learn to communicate with others more effectively and authentically, we want to explore effective and collaborative ways to express benevolent leadership to our animal companions.

Leaders in Nature

Dogs live in social groups and establish hierarchies to maintain order and cooperation. In nature, the pack leader is consistent and assertive, clearly setting the tone for what is expected and acceptable pack behavior. Leadership is not about dominance or aggression but about predictable, stable, and balanced energy. Leaders of the pack rule benevolently, creating a secure, steady social order. Leadership is essential to provide direction and alleviate stress for your dog. If a void in leadership exists, your pup may assume the role, leading to anxiety or territorial behavior.

Effective Leadership

Leadership can and should be earned without physical dominance or aggressive training. To be an effective leader, set clear boundaries and give constant feedback. Your pup should earn everything, from treats to cuddles, through commands, building confidence, and good decision-making skills. Acknowledging your pup's emotions and experiences and providing guidance in new situations will help foster a dynamic and confident companion. Avoid giving your dog complete control over the house, and don't use baby talk or excessive cuddling, as higher pitches and overly attentive energy can signal you are not confident enough to be in charge and need to be protected. It can also lead to increased separation anxiety. By having your dog earn rewards and consistently reinforcing good behavior, you establish yourself as the benevolent leader, creating open communication and a trusting bond with your pup.

Do

- Let your dog know what behaviors you like and consistently redirect any behavior you don't to avoid confusion and build trust.
- Give food, praise, and attention only when your dog is calm and collaborative.
- Claim as your own anything your dog values, including toys or different areas of the house.
- Get a command before setting down your dog's food bowl.
- Enter and exit thresholds before your dog.
- Lead by example, modeling the energy you want to see from your dog.

Do Not

- Give your dog the run of the house.
- Allow your dog to have free access to toys.
- Engage every time your dog brings you a toy.
- Continue bargaining or asking for a command your dog is confused by or ignoring.
- Use a high-pitched voice or baby voice.
- Speak in anger.

Troubleshooting

Finding Your Authentic Style. Discovering our unique leadership style is paramount for effective training, communication, and connection. Both animal companions and pet parents have unique personalities and tendencies. While a husband may excel with a commanding presence, leveraging his physical attributes like broad shoulders and a deep voice, attempting to mimic his approach might feel forced for his wife. Each individual, regardless of gender, possesses distinct strengths. For the wife, authenticity may lie in a leadership style grounded in collaboration and gentle assertiveness. Recognizing and embracing one's unique strengths not only fosters a harmonious relationship with the pet but also cultivates an environment where diverse leadership styles can coexist, enhancing the overall training experience.

Additional Considerations

Trusting Your Voice. Many of us can be critical of how our voices sound or the missteps we may make with our words. It is powerful to speak our truth and communicate, trusting that the energy and vibration of our words will project authentically, even if we stumble on our words. When we uncover and speak our truth in every area of our lives, we inspire others to find their voice, too. An important distinction is that we do not speak our truth because we want it to be heard and agreed with by everyone—we speak up because of our passion and convictions, and we are secure enough in it that we do not need to defend it, impose it on others, or be militant. Rather, we share our words in love and authenticity and in the hope that they will reach those who benefit from hearing them.

Feeling Heard. Feeling heard begins with ourselves. If we feel we are not being heard by others or by our pet during training, it could be because we are not valuing, trusting, or listening to our own inner voice. Pet training is an opportunity to practice getting clear on how we are communicating with our pet, making sure our energy is matching the request. As we do, clear and cohesive communication becomes second nature, and we become more compelling to our pets and other humans in our lives. And as a result, our message is more often received, or we develop a better idea of who truly listens to us and who does not. This way, we avoid wasting our breath or taking not being heard by that individual personally. If you catch yourself repeatedly asking for the same command and your furry friend is ignoring you, ask clearly for what you want, but be prepared to walk away if you don't get it. Return after a few seconds to restate your terms (ask for the command), and you will find that you are much more persuasive than if you had bargained with your pup.

Following Your Truth. While professionals may offer valuable insights into general training techniques, pet parents are the true experts in understanding the nuances of their specific pets and the dynamics within their familial pack. So, although you may be seeking out experts in dog training, you are the expert when it comes to your pet. It's paramount to trust your instincts and inner voice when expert advice doesn't align with your or your pet's personality, your leadership style, or the established pack dynamic. In such instances, take charge by voicing your concerns and collaboratively work with experts to tailor solutions that resonate authentically with your pet's disposition and your own preferences, rejecting generic approaches in favor of a customized training strategy that feels more authentic for the dynamic you share with your pet.

CASE STUDIES

Case Study #1

The Profound Influence of Words

As we learn how best to communicate, we develop and cultivate a "Voice." Sometimes, we forget that our voice is a powerful tool, even when used in jest. This case underscores how important it is to intentionally choose our words with care and sincerity.

Our animal companions lack the capacity to grasp sarcasm, self-deprecating humor, or dry wit, so they often respond to our words and energy with pure sincerity.

One particular pet parent I worked with had a furry duo that brought immense joy to her life. Yet, in jest, she often quipped about the hectic nature of her days, suggesting that she'd be "*the luckiest woman in the world*" if she woke up to find that one of her pups had run away. Her playful banter wasn't a reflection of how she truly felt about her furry companions, but her words carried unexpected gravitas.

One Saturday morning, her joke transformed into reality. A desperate phone call reached me as she frantically reported that one of her dogs was missing. The pet parent was devastated at the prospect of her sarcastic quips being taken earnestly by the pet she cherished and adored. She was remorseful and desperate to have her furry friend back in her arms.

Hours later, the pup was discovered in the stairwell of her building, just one floor down from the back door entrance to her apartment. The dog was safe and carefree, but the pet parent was understandably shaken. The incident served as an eye-opening revelation, emphasizing how her pet had taken her harmless jokes and dry humor quite literally.

This episode brought to light the influence of our words and the weight they carry. Each utterance can shape our beliefs, experiences, relationships, and very real outcomes. At the core of humor often lies a kernel of truth, and our pets don't always discriminate when it comes to the energy and intent behind our words.

What had started off as a joke was parlayed into a serious priority. I worked with the pet parent to establish protocol and resources to relieve any underlying stress associated with caring for her pets on particularly busy days. And while, of course, the pet parent wanted her beloved furry companions always by her side, she was grateful to have dog walkers and daycares on hand.

Practical Insight: Be mindful of the words you choose, as they hold the potential to shape your reality. Your voice matters, and every utterance has the power to manifest your intentions. Whether directed at your beloved pets, the universe, or even yourself, let your words be a source of love, positivity, and authentic expression.

Case Study #2:
"Who's Walking Whom?"

This case study underscores how our training challenges can mirror broader insecurities, and the profound impact aligning pet training methods with our authentic self and tendencies can have in other areas of our lives.

A woman reached out for help working on her pet's on-leash etiquette. Her pet zig-zagged and chose his own path on leash despite the pet parent trying to set the tone, pace, and direction.

As we walked down the block, the conversation turned toward her job responsibilities. She worked in a predominantly male industry and recently was put in a managerial position she didn't feel equipped to handle. The pet parent already felt as if she was never respected or listened to when it came to her personal life and career, so the thought of trying to lead a lively, rambunctious Australian Shepherd mix on a leash, given all other stresses in her life was an anxiety-inducing prospect that added to her self-doubt and feelings of inadequacy.

Yet, here she was, with her beloved dog by her side, determined to master the art of walking on leash and stepping into a leadership role. A task that might seem mundane took on profound meaning for this pet parent. It wasn't just about the leash; it was about the confidence she wanted to exude in her leadership and ability to guide and protect.

As the session continued, a passerby couldn't resist commenting, "*Who's walking who?*" It was lighthearted in its intent but struck a nerve deep within the pet parent.

It wasn't just about the leash, her dog, or the on-leash etiquette. It was a mirror reflecting her deepest insecurities and doubts. The phrase echoed her internal monologue of not being good or strong enough to lead her dog, let alone a challenging team at work.

But she had embarked on a journey of personal growth alongside her canine friend. She was resolute in her pursuit of self-discovery and transformation. Each step they took together was a testament to her unwavering commitment to becoming the leader she aspired to be. The leash wasn't just a tether to her dog but a lifeline connecting her to her own strength.

Her desire to be confident and respected resulted in a thirst for corporate leadership books. The pet parent understood the many ways adopting and embodying these principles would apply not only to her career but her personal life as well. As the pet parent's pursuits in corporate management progressed, so did her confidence in leading her furry friend on leash. Despite the tailspin that one observation caused, she grew to trust that through her commitment to uncovering her authentic leadership style, she now had the voice and confidence to respond to any comment, whether in the board room or out and about with her pup.

Practical Insight: The next time you encounter someone grappling with their leash and their own internal struggles, remember the power your words hold. Instead of questioning, offer encouragement and acknowledgment. The challenges we face on leash often mirror the battles we fight within ourselves. Kindness and positivity can be the beacon of light they need on their journey, inspiring confidence, strengthening bonds, and fostering shared victories.

Activities

CLAIMING NEW HABITS

Voice Intentions. Start your day by setting clear intentions for being grounded and present. Remind yourself of these intentions throughout the day, reinforcing your commitment to fully engaging in your experiences.

Chasing Down Experiences. Exploring new environments, tastes, smells, and sensations helps keep your furry friend stimulated, curious, happy, and confident. The same applies for us. Although it's easy to stick with our habitual routine, relationships, and rhythm, it's important to change things up and explore the world. In that mindset of exploration, we can bridge gaps, mend fences, understand perspectives, and put ourselves in others' shoes—all things that make us more insightful and empathic pet parents.

COME COMMAND TRAINING

The idea is to teach your dog to willingly and quickly command, whether indoors during playtime, outdoors any time he may be faced with a potentially hazardous

1. Either have someone hold your dog's harness, or, if alone, put your dog in a SIT/STAY. Place your baited hand in front of your dog's nose so she can smell the treat and you have her attention. Then, back away from your dog, about three feet to start.
2. In a happy and inviting tone, call your dog's name, and when she is looking at you, excitedly say the verbal cue "COME!" with a big Touch hand gesture.
3. When your dog approaches you, reach under her chin to gently grab her harness, and when you have a hold of it, mark it with a YES, treat, and praise lavishly.
4. If reaching for your dog's harness makes her retreat, use a treat to lure her toward you, distracting her while you take hold of the harness. When you have a hold of it, mark it with a YES, treat, and praise lavishly.
5. Repeat the above step 3-5 times, stepping farther away each time so that your dog must cover greater distances to reach you.
6. Begin calling your dog's name and asking her to "COME!" without first approaching your dog to let her smell the treat.

BUILDING THE COME COMMAND

Wean out the treats first through delaying rewards and then via an intermittent schedule of reinforcement. Always reward better performances with higher-value treats.

Reinforce this task by calling your puppy multiple times daily, giving a cuddle or treat, and sending him on his way. This will help him learn that by coming to you, good things happen.

Once your dog can perform the COME command consistently without distraction indoors, practice the command in different places different distractions (e.g., in hallways, indoors around other dogs, at a fenced-in dog park).

Rules of Paw

- Avoid calling your puppy to you only to bring her inside, put her in her crate, or otherwise end something fun. Never call your puppy to you for discipline.
- Because it is essential that COME be a fun command, ensure that each training session is simple and pleasurable by always resulting in success.
- If you are practicing outdoors where your dog could escape, have her wear a lightweight, long leash (which can be left dangling as your dog wanders and investigates).

HOUSEBREAKING, ACCIDENTS
& Leading an Intentional Life

OVERVIEW

Shared Motivation
Esteem Needs for Being Regarded by Others

Energetic Overlay
Sixth Chakra affecting Sinuses and Eyes

Universal Themes
Acknowledgment, Regard, Perception, Vision, Expectations,
Disappointment & Being Intentional

Translating Your Pet's Behavior
Where are you feeling disregarded, disappointed, or pissed off?
Where are you not acknowledging a situation or relationship
for what it truly is?
Are there big releases in your life you could more intentionally clear?
Where are you energetically soiling things in your life?

Housebreaking

Whether teaching your pup to use the wee wee pad or eliminate outside, housebreaking requires patience and a plan. The notion of elimination can also help us be more intentional about what we want to release in our lives. As we translate our pet's behavior, we will explore matters associated with the sixth chakra of acknowledgment, perception, vision, expectations, disappointment & being intentional.

What Is Housebreaking?

Housebreaking in pet training relates to the process of teaching pets, particularly puppies, appropriate bathroom habits. Accidents refer to instances when a pet relieves themselves somewhere inappropriate, which can be frustrating for pet parents. A structured training approach helps pets understand where it's acceptable to eliminate, whether indoors on a wee wee pad, outdoors, or both. Effective housebreaking relies on consistent schedules, positive reinforcement for going in the designated area, and patience. Over time, pets learn to follow the desired bathroom routine, ensuring a clean and comfortable living environment for both pets and their humans.

UNDERSTANDING MOTIVATION

When your pet has accidents or struggles with housebreaking—or you or your pet is experiencing issues with eyes, sight, or sinuses—it is an opportunity to explore matters related to feeling regarded, perception, your expectations versus reality, acknowledgment, disappointment, and trusting your vision and intuition. Consider how these factors influence your pet's behavior and how they relate to your own feelings about the situation.

Parallel in Maslow's Pyramid: Esteem Needs for Being Regarded by Others

In Maslow's Hierarchy of Needs, our esteem needs include a desire to be acknowledged, positively regarded, and taken into consideration by others. Accidents and housebreaking issues with our pets tap into the disappointment of feeling disregarded or not having our expectations met. Our pet's accidents prompt us to face the reality of situations and relationships we may be avoiding, and see them for what they truly are. Just like us, our pets desire to be held in high regard by their pack and feel accidents and setbacks in housebreaking may affect how you regard them.

Parallel in the Chakra System: Sixth Chakra

Balancing the sixth chakra is essential for developing our inner wisdom and improving insight, vision, and clarity on situations and dynamics. Meditation and visualization exercises can help bring the sixth chakra into alignment, leading to a heightened sense of intuition and a stronger vision for the life we want to share with our pets.

Signs It's In Balance

- Strong sense of inner guidance.
- Open to unusual perspectives.
- Making decisions based on a clear vision.
- Strong insight, self-awareness, and ability to perceive hidden truths.

Signs It's Out of Balance

- Difficulty in trusting one's intuition or vision.
- Overactive imagination or constantly daydreaming.
- Issues with concentration or memory.
- Being short-sighted about dynamics, situations, or opportunities.
- Physical issues affecting sinuses or eyes.

Unique Themes Attributed to the Sixth Chakra

Intuition and Perception: Closely associated with heightened intuition and the ability to perceive the world beyond the physical senses.

Inner Wisdom: Governs insight, allowing us to tap into our intuition and vision.

Visualization and Imagination: Linked to the power of the mind's eye to create and manifest.

Awareness and Mindfulness: Emphasizes the importance of intentionality in our daily lives.

Acceptance. Linked to acceptance of past and current dynamics, understanding what can and cannot be changed.

THE MINDSET SHIFT

Understanding these mindset shifts can lead to a more successful housebreaking process, strengthen the bond between you and your pet, and have a positive effect across various areas of your life.

Mindset Shift with Housebreaking

Going from feeling disregarded and disappointed by your pet's accidents *to* accepting that accidents happen and with consistent routines, positive reinforcement, and efforts to lead a more intentional life, you can foster a clearer, more harmonious living space for you and your animal companion.

Mindset Shift in Other Areas of Our Lives

Going From Limiting Mindsets Like >>

Having rigid perspectives

Having unrealistic expectations

Having no sense of humor

Being hard-headed

Maintaining that seeing is believing

Being naïve

Often feeling let down

Being avoidant

Feeling misunderstood or disregarded

Remaining bitter about the past

Experiencing no harmony in the home or relationships

Showing up in limiting mindsets like:

I do not feel seen for who I truly am.

I do not want to see others or situations for what they are.

I do not want to see other points of view or criticisms.

I do not see my life playing out as I had expected it to.

I do not want to face annoyances or grievances.

Going To Beneficial Mindsets Like >>

Being a visionary

Experiencing harmony in home and relationships

Being forgiving

Seeing situations and relationships for what they are

Using intuition to navigate situations

Enjoying good debate and new perspectives

Acting as a good mediator

Having a clear vision for your life

Playing the hand that is dealt without simply wishing things were different

Showing up in beneficial mindsets like:

I am seen for who I truly am by those who matter the most.

I accept reality as it is and make decisions based on informed perceptions.

Other points of view and constructive criticism contribute to my personal growth.

I accept my reality as it unfolds and see opportunities within unexpected outcomes.

I see challenges as stepping stones for a better future.

TRANSLATING YOUR PET'S BEHAVIOR

Housebreaking issues can help us grow if we are intentional about our expectations and how we process our own energies around the successes as well as the disappointments. Housebreaking issues are grounded in the sixth chakra, which includes matters dealing with illusion vs. reality, seeing things for what they truly are, our family dynamic, and our relationships through others' eyes.

> *Where are you feeling disregarded, disappointed, or 'pissed off'?*
> *Is your pet acting as a proxy for a larger release occurring?*
> *Where are you not acknowledging a situation or relationship for what it truly is?*
> *Where are you energetically soiling things in your life?*

Where are you feeling disregarded, disappointed, or 'pissed off'?
Whether in housebreaking or other aspects of life, we can feel disenchanted when our expectations differ from reality. When we avoid facing feelings of being disregarded, disappointed, disillusioned, or aggravated, it not only limits us in life but is energetically draining. More than mere accidents, our pets' messes can mirror deeper emotional turmoil and unaddressed annoyances.

Practical Insight: Acknowledge areas in your life where you feel disregarded, have unrealistic expectations, or are holding on to past disappointments that limit you. Seek to accept circumstances and dynamics you cannot change. Trust your intuition and vision to let annoyances go, find resolution, and engage in intentional ways forward for the benefit of both you and your pet.

Is your animal companion acting as a proxy for a larger cleanse or release that is occurring?

Have you been processing a relationship, experience, trauma, or realization? Have you been clearing the energies of your home, but you're not being intentional about how you are releasing and transmuting it? Allowing external energies to accumulate during big emotional clearings can clutter, overload, and compromise our energetic fields. If we are experiencing any significant emotional or mental clearings in our lives, including releasing hurts, unrealistic expectations, disappointments, or stories, regular cleansing of our energetic field is essential. If not, our animal companion may process that energy on our behalf, showing up in the form of accidents.

Practical Insight: During emotional or energetic cleansing, focus on the intentional release and transmutation of nonbeneficial energies. Replace them with harmonious and loving vibrations to maintain a balanced and peaceful environment for you and your animal companion.

Where are you not accepting a situation or relationship for what it truly is?

When your pet has an accident, it cannot be disregarded. The mess needs to be addressed right away. However, in other areas of our lives, we try to avoid messy dynamics in relationships and careers by ignoring red flags or overlooking uncomfortable truths. We do so to avoid facing accumulated emotional baggage, unrealistic expectations, and past or future disappointments. Our pets invite us to face reality, even if it's uncomfortable. This honesty can lead to more constructive ways forward and healthier relationships.

Practical Insight: Be mindful of situations or relationships where you might avoid seeing reality. Just as a pet's accident can reflect avoidance or denial playing out in your life, humans can sometimes overlook uncomfortable truths. Seek the perspective of trusted friends or family as input to help you sort through your perception of the situation, and align on a strategy to more intentionally move forward. Challenge yourself to face and accept the reality of the situation, even if it's difficult, and take appropriate actions.

Where are you energetically soiling things in your life?
Where are you releasing energy, expelling, or venting in inappropriate ways? Is there a better way to handle those energies and emotions? Are you addressing the core issue, or are you gossiping or acting on unresolved feelings about a person or situation, like telling the same story over and over again? Just as we need to effectively clean up messes when our pets have an accidental elimination, we need to be intentional about properly clearing energy and mindsets rather than releasing and expelling them in inappropriate ways. Cultivating this habit of intentional clearing frees up mental and emotional space for positive growth.

Practical Insight: Be intentional about letting go of these burdens and stories that no longer serve you. When you catch yourself venting or dumping emotional baggage on a friend, pause and consider if there's a more constructive way to handle your emotions. Redirect your energy into a creative pursuit, journaling, exercise, or meditation, and reward yourself for finding healthier outlets.

HOUSEBREAKING TRAINING

Housebreaking a puppy requires understanding their elimination patterns and setting up a schedule. Monitoring food and water intake helps predict elimination times.

When away from home, use a crate or confinement area. Puppies instinctively avoid soiling their sleeping area. However, for young puppies, limit crate time to 2-3 hour stretches to avoid accidents. Supervise puppies constantly, watch for signs of needing to eliminate, and reward good behavior.

Because proper bathroom habits are essential to a harmonious living environment with your pet, let's explore some techniques to help you set your pet up for success.

Indoor vs. Outdoor Elimination

Wee wee pads are useful for indoor training, and eventually, you can train your pet to go outside exclusively by using better treats to reward eliminating outdoors. Leveraging high-value treats outside and less exciting treats indoors for eliminating on the wee wee pad makes "going" outdoors more rewarding for your pet. When given the option, they will "hold it" until they are outdoors to receive the more motivating treat.

Establishing a Routine

A consistent routine is crucial for house training and following these steps can help:

- **Feeding Schedule.** Set a regular feeding schedule for your pet, providing meals at the same times each day. This helps regulate their digestion and establishes a predictable bathroom routine.

- **Potty Breaks.** Take your pet outside for potty breaks at regular intervals, such as after meals, naps, playtime, or waking up from sleep. This helps them associate specific times with going to the bathroom.
- **Designated Elimination Area.** Choose a specific area in your yard or a nearby outdoor location where you want your pet to eliminate. Take them to this spot consistently to reinforce the association between that area and bathroom behavior.

Supervision and Rewards

Supervision plays a crucial role in preventing accidents and reinforcing desired bathroom behaviors. Follow these steps to effectively supervise and reward your pet during house training:

- Leash your pet or keep them within sight when indoors to monitor their behavior and anticipate signs that they need to eliminate.
- Immediately take your pet to the designated elimination area when you notice signs such as sniffing, circling, or restlessness.
- Use a verbal cue such as "go potty" or "bombs away" to associate the command with the desired behavior.
- When your pet eliminates in the designated area, offer immediate praise, treats, and positive reinforcement to reinforce the behavior.

Troubleshooting

Stay Calm. If you catch your pet in the act of eliminating indoors, do not startle to interrupt, punish, or scold them, as this may create confusion or fear of eliminating in front of you.

Clean Thoroughly. Clean any accidents promptly and thoroughly using an enzymatic cleaner specifically designed to remove pet odors.

This helps eliminate residual smells that may attract your pet to eliminate in the same spot again.

Adjust the Routine. If accidents occur frequently, consider adjusting the routine. Take your pet out for potty breaks more frequently, provide closer supervision, and reinforce positive bathroom behaviors more consistently. If accidents are consistently happening in the same place, block access to that spot and keep an eye out for your dog sniffing in that area. This may be a clue that they need to eliminate, so taking them to a more appropriate area can help them succeed.

Health Concerns. If your puppy or mature companion is having a lot of small accidents around the house, it may be a sign of stress, marking, or a urinary tract infection, so always check with your vet to discard the latter as an option.

Remove the Temptation. Sometimes, our pets do the unthinkable—they eat poop. This can occur for various reasons: 1) medical issues like parasites or lack of nutrients, 2) with a rich diet, their poop may smell as good coming out as it did going in, and 3) the way we rush to pick it up makes it seem incredibly valuable, so they endeavor to get to it first. Although unpleasant, understanding what motivates the behavior is important to address it effectively. It is important to rule out medical concerns, so consult your vet on whether a check-up is needed. If the smell is attracting your pet, consider sliced pineapples or enzyme formulas that can act as a deterrent. And finally, if your furry friend perceives it to be valuable, given your enthusiasm to pick it up, ask for a redirective command like a Touch to get your furry friend away from the temptation and toss a treat in the opposite direction. This will buy you time to calmly clean up the area.

Additional Considerations

Feeling Disregarded. Housebreaking is by far one of the more emotionally triggering experiences for pet parents. Accidents remind us that our world is not perfect and that unexpected accidents can happen and soil an otherwise flawless rug. The mindset that our puppy is eliminating in inappropriate places out of spite or that he knows better strikes a chord that makes us feel disrespected and disregarded. The energy of disappointment around housebreaking and attaching anxiety and resentment to the act of our puppy eliminating in front of us can actually slow down the process. Remember that accidents are a normal part of the process, and progress may take time. By establishing a routine, providing supervision, and rewarding desired behaviors, we can help our pet develop good bathroom habits.

Keep the Dog, Drop the Dogma. In housebreaking and pet care, more generally, there's wisdom in embracing a flexible and open-minded approach. Our pets remind us to let go of rigid expectations, mindsets, and one-size-fits-all training techniques. In recognizing that our pets are unique individuals with their own personalities and needs, it becomes evident that strict adherence to dogmatic rules does not serve their best interests. Avoid deeply ingrained mindsets about pet behavior or popular training methods that don't work for your specific companion. Being open to new thinking and perspectives can lead to more harmonious and effective interactions with our furry friends.

Living Intentionally. Just like our physical bodies, our energetic bodies demand proper care and maintenance. Our energetic fields become overloaded with vibrations that do not belong to us. This can lead to fatigue, depression, anxiety, mood swings, and poor eating and sleeping habits for us and our pets. Eventually, this can even lead to pain, dysfunction, and disease within the physical body.

Allowing external energies to accumulate within us can clutter, overload, and compromise our energetic fields. Regularly cleansing our energy is essential. When we neglect this responsibility, our pets might shoulder the burden. This can lead to accidents as they clear the energy the only way they know how, like eliminating inappropriately.

Yet, let's not stop there. To achieve a holistic sense of well-being, we must also consider the energy in physical environments and their impact on us and our animal companions. The energetic cleanliness of our spaces is pivotal in sustaining well-being for us and our furry friends. The simple act of decluttering and organizing can bring more clarity and harmony to your home, helping with the housebreaking process.

Visualization is a powerful tool; you can visualize your space filled with love, peace, calmness, relaxation, and harmony. Sage burning may be too intense for your pet's sensitive nose, so briefly opening windows daily or strategically placing crystals around your home may be a better option. Ringing a singing bowl can also help maintain light and flowing energies in your living space. Be it objects, furniture, broadcasts, energies, emotions, or people, it benefits you and your pets when you regularly declutter your space and are intentional about what you allow to remain or return.

Unlocking Vision. Unlike our animal companions, we humans don't always trust our instincts about situations, dynamics, and relationships. Our pets help us remember the importance of observing each situation free from expectations or preconceptions and listening to our intuition to decide how to proceed. Trusting our inner guidance not only helps us be clear on the energy surrounding us but also helps us be a better pet parent. By regularly listening to our own intuition, we become confident in our discernment of what is best for our furry friend in terms of their training, healthcare, and emotional needs.

CASE STUDIES

Case Study #1

Housebreaking as a Reflection of Inner Turmoil

Merlin's story reminds us of the importance of listening to our pets' behaviors, which, when acknowledged, can lead to transformative changes for the entire pack. More than mere accidents, Merlin's housebreaking issues were prompting his pet parent to take a deeper look at her romantic partner. The results were life-changing for both Merlin and his human counterpart.

Merlin's pet parent, a successful and dynamic individual in her social and professional life, faced a pivotal crossroads in her journey. She had found a potential life partner, a decision that carried significant weight as she contemplated starting a family. However, deep down, she recognized certain aspects of this man that were fundamentally misaligned with her core values and the vision she held for her life. Fearing time was running out, she contemplated settling for him, convincing herself that "*nobody's perfect.*"

Merlin, sensitive to the emotional undercurrents surrounding him, expressed his concern in a unique way— through housebreaking accidents, but with a specific target: the side of the bed where her boyfriend slept. Rather than a mere male standoff, Merlin's actions reflected his pet parent's internal struggle. He sought to communicate a truth she already knew but had been reluctant to confront.

Merlin's strategy was effective and prompted his pet parent to address her hesitation to see the situation for what it truly was, to acknowledge that the reality of her relationship was not aligning with her expectations, and to confront the red flags she had pushed aside.

Realizing that no member of the pack could continue suppressing these very real concerns, Merlin's parent made a transformative decision to break up with the man she was unsure about. In doing so, she created space for a more fitting romantic relationship to enter her life, and not long after, they joyfully welcomed a baby girl.

Practical Insight: Merlin's story serves as a poignant reminder of how our pets can help us confront our inner truths and guide us toward the path that aligns more fully with the vision for our lives, ultimately leading to fulfillment and happiness.

Case Study #2
Breaking the Cycle

When it comes to housebreaking our pets, accidents happen, and one aspect that might leave pet parents puzzled and understandably squeamish is the peculiar behavior of their dog eating their own excrement. And in this particular case, the less-than-appealing behavior uncovered an unsavory parallel in his pet parent's life.

In this story, a woman sought my guidance because her beloved pet was engaging in a new, less-than-appetizing behavior: he had developed a propensity to consume his own excrement. This unsettling habit had left her perplexed, as she had tried various strategies, from redirective training to digestive powders, with no success in curbing the behavior.

After an intuitive reading with her, it became evident that there was more to this behavior. A parallel between her dog's unpalatable habit and her own life choices was revealed.

This pet parent had recently separated from her husband, and though they lived apart, he still contributed to household expenses, which left her feeling obligated to him. The pet parent recognized that, much like her canine companion, she had been swallowing her own metaphorical "poop." She was allowing herself to be on the receiving end of her ex-husband's rants and demands. Since he was providing financial support, she felt it was something she had to endure, even when it was detrimental to her emotional well-being. And that realization left her with a bitter aftertaste.

With the epiphany that her actions and her pet's behavior were connected, she became more intentional in her interactions with her ex-husband. She was clear on what she would tolerate and what she would no longer accept in terms of his words and energetic dumping. And as she cleaned up her act in terms of not allowing her ex-husband to freely soil her energy, so did her dog. The habit of eating his own excrement gradually waned and eventually ceased, mirroring his pet parent's own newfound strength and determination to break the cycle of metaphorically ingesting what others indiscriminately eliminate.

Practical Insight: Just as this pet parent acknowledged it was time to break free from the destructive cycle of accommodating unpleasant dynamics, our pets remind us to be more mindful and intentional about what we're willing to accept, as we all too often energetically take on and digest what others release.

Scan this QR code to access an hour-by-hour suggested schedule for housebreaking a puppy.

Activities

3 SPRING CLEANING IDEAS FOR YOUR PETS

Pup-dating Contacts. Collect and review all of your pet-related business cards to create a one-sheeter of VIP names and contact information, such as your animal companion's vet, sitter, groomer, and favorite puppy playmates, along with 24-hour emergency pet hospitals and pet-friendly hotels in your area. Consolidate all your pet-related receipts in a folder to share with your accountant for potential deductions come tax time.

Cleanliness is Next to Dogliness. Check expiration dates and safely discard treats, medications, and dental or grooming products that are no longer valid. Bacteria can form on your dog's toys over time, so set the goal of cleaning and sanitizing them regularly in your dishwasher or microwave using natural cleaning products.

Go with the Flow. Visualize your space filled with love, peace, calm, relaxation, and bliss to help set a mood in which your pup wants to luxuriate. Opening windows for 15 minutes a day, strategically placing crystals, or even clapping can help keep the energies in your home light and flowing. Clear the energy in your house regularly or enlist the help of a Space Clearing Specialist.

LEAVE IT COMMAND TRAINING

The idea is to condition your dog to leave whatever appealing item they are going after and look to you instead. Whether it is food in the kitchen, a cigarette butt on the street, or the legs of your favorite chair, Leave It is an important and potentially life-saving command to help your dog understand that a particular item is off-limits.

1. Kneel in front of your dog, place an average treat in your hand, and make a fist.
2. Place your baited fist in front of your dog's nose and then flush on the floor so they can smell the treat and begin sniffing and potentially even pawing at it.
3. The instant your dog backs off and stops trying to get at the treat, mark it with a YES or CLICK if clicker training and use a higher-value treat to reward your dog.
4. Repeat this exercise 7 to 10 times until your dog consistently ignores the treat and looks at you.
5. Show your dog the average treat again, and now stand and cover it with your foot. Again, wait until your dog stops trying to get the treat. The instant they back off, mark it with a YES and use a higher-value treat to reward your dog. If your dog refuses to go after the treat altogether, jackpot him/her.
6. Repeat this exercise 7 to 10 times until your dog consistently ignores the treat and looks at you.
7. Toss the average treat on the floor right next to your foot, where you can cover it quickly if your dog dives for it. Add the verbal cue "LEAVE IT."
8. If he/she goes for the treat, cover it with your foot, wait for your dog to back off, mark it with a YES, and use a higher-value treat to reward your dog. If they refuse to go after the treat altogether, jackpot your dog with multiple treats as a reward.

BUILDING THE LEAVE IT COMMAND

Wean out the treats first through delaying rewards and then via an intermittent schedule of reinforcement. Always reward better performances with higher-value treats.

Once your dog can perform the LEAVE IT command without distractions indoors, practice the command in different places with different distractions (i.e., in the elevator, outdoors).

As you continue training, challenge your dog a bit more by asking him or her to Leave different treats or objects. Move the treat around with your foot. Drop it from a few inches up, then from table height, or toss it gently in their direction.

Practice asking your dog to Leave an item within a lineup of items he/she can have to add in the element of foraging and surprise.

DROP IT COMMAND TRAINING

The idea is to condition your dog to drop whatever appealing item they have in their mouth. Whether it is a cigarette butt on the street or simply your pup's favorite toy during fetch, Drop It is a dynamic command which can be fun but also potentially life-saving.

1. Kneel in front of your dog, and offer your pup one of his favorite toys. Wait for him/her to take hold of it.
2. Still keeping hold of the toy, place your baited fist in front of your dog's nose so they can smell the treat.
3. The instant your dog releases the toy to get at the treat, mark it with a YES or CLICK if clicker training, and then treat and praise your dog. If your dog does not let go of the toy, try wiggling the treat or holding it closer to his/her nose, or try using a less exciting toy or treat combination until your pup gets the hang of it.
4. Repeat this exercise 7-10x until your dog quickly gives up control of the toy when they see your fist.
5. Crouch in front of your dog and offer them a toy, allowing your pup to have full control of it. Put out your fist and add the verbal cue "DROP IT." If your dog releases the toy, mark it with a YES and jackpot him/her.
6. Repeat this exercise 7-10 times until your dog quickly releases it when they see your fist. Gradually begin holding your fist farther away from your pup's nose, working up to a standing position. Try the command without the treat, praising your dog if he/she complies.

BUILDING THE DROP IT COMMAND

Wean out the treats first through delaying rewards and then via an intermittent schedule of reinforcement. Always reward better performances with higher-value treats.

Once your dog can perform the DROP IT command without distractions indoors, practice the command in different places (i.e., in the elevator, outdoors) with different toys and items.

MOMENTS OF CRISIS
& Understanding the Big Picture

OVERVIEW

Shared Motivation
Self-Fulfillment Needs of Self-Actualization

Energetic Overlay
Seventh Chakra affecting the Brain

Universal Themes
Surrender, Transcendence, Spirituality, Purpose,
Doubt & Faith in Moments of Crisis

Translating Your Pet's Behavior

What new abilities or insights are emerging as a response to this crisis?

What possibilities open up if you look at the bigger picture?

What other relationships or experiences in your life have transcended the physical?

What does this current crisis illuminate about past grief or difficult situations?

Where else in your life could you have more faith?

Sick, Lost & Transitioned Pets

Understanding our role in the universe has intrigued humanity since the dawn of time. Let's explore the multi-faceted role we play in our pet's life, in our family, in our community, and in the collective. We'll reflect on how moments of crisis can serve as an opportunity to re-examine and recommit to our beliefs and truths and realize our impact in this world is bigger than the sum of our parts.

What Are Moments of Crisis?

Moments of crisis with a pet encompass emotionally challenging situations, such as having a pet go missing, a pet getting sick, or dealing with the loss of a beloved pet that has passed away. These experiences can be incredibly distressing for pet parents, often unleashing a complex mix of emotions. When a pet goes missing, there's an overwhelming sense of worry, fear, and helplessness as we search and hope for their safe return. In the case of a pet crossing over, grief and loss can trigger a profound sense of sadness and, at times, even guilt. These moments of crisis highlight the deep emotional bonds we share with our pets and the intense love and care that we invest in them. Coping with these situations often involves reaching out for support from friends, family, or pet support groups to navigate the complex emotions that arise during such challenging times.

UNDERSTANDING MOTIVATION

When your pet is ill, missing, or has crossed over—or either you or your pet are experiencing issues with the brain—it is an opportunity to explore matters related to understanding the bigger picture and having faith in moments of crisis. Consider how these factors influence your perception of the situation and your pet's journey.

Parallel in Maslow's Pyramid: Self-Fulfillment Needs of Self-Actualization

Maslow's Hierarchy frames self-fulfillment needs in terms of our desire to actualize and achieve our full potential. Our pets share this aspiration, and when they go missing or face serious health challenges, these situations can help them fulfill their purpose. These moments of crisis can be opportunities for them to be part of experiences that contribute to their own self-actualization, which often help us step more fully into our own as well. Even if it is difficult for us to comprehend in the moment, their journey may offer an opportunity for us to explore a new role as a caretaker, healer, and source of support.

Parallel in the Chakra System: Seventh Chakra

We can enjoy a higher state of awareness and a profound sense of interconnectedness with all of existence by balancing the seventh chakra. Practices like meditation, prayer, and contemplation can help bring this chakra into alignment, leading to a heightened sense of spiritual awareness, integration of all aspects of self, and unity with the universe.

Signs It's In Balance

- Experiencing a deep sense of spiritual connection and oneness with the universe.
- Feeling a profound sense of peace and contentment.
- Having a clear understanding of one's life purpose and spiritual path.
- Embracing a sense of surrender and trust in the flow of life.

Signs It's Out of Balance

- Feeling disconnected from spirituality or struggling with doubts and skepticism.
- Experiencing a lack of purpose or feeling lost in life.
- Being excessively attached to material possessions or achievements.
- Suffering from a sense of spiritual arrogance or superiority.
- Physical symptoms involving the brain, such as headaches and brain fog.

Unique Themes Attributed to the Seventh Chakra

Spiritual Connection: Closely associated with the direct connection to the "divine" and the universal consciousness.

Transcendence and Enlightenment: Governs the ability to transcend the limitations of the ego.

Higher Consciousness: Represents the highest states of consciousness and the integration of all chakras.

Universal Wisdom: Linked to the wisdom and guidance that comes from connecting with the universal source.

Surrender and Trust: Emphasizes the importance of surrendering to the flow of life and trusting in the higher plan.

THE MINDSET SHIFT

Having faith in moments of crisis is essential. Trust that your pet is on their personal path of transformation and that you have played an important role in their life. It is a moment to believe in the potential for growth and self-actualization for both you and your pet, even in the face of challenging circumstances.

Mindset Shift with Moments of Crisis

Going from feeling overwhelmed by emotions and a sense of responsibility for your pet's condition during crises *to* the realization that these moments offer an opportunity for your pet to help you step into a more powerful and purposeful role and a deeper, new way to connect with them.

Mindset Shift in Other Areas of Our Lives

Going From Limiting Mindsets Like >>

Overthinking

Being a know-it-all

Being narrow-minded

Having paralysis by analysis

Needing proof to believe

Being self-absorbed and self-centered

Believing there is nothing more than meets the eye

Being jaded and fatalistic

Seeing everything as separate and independent

Failing to understand patterns

Showing up in limiting mindsets like:

I do not understand how each part contributes to the whole.

I feel misunderstood or not at home in the universe.

I do not understand or have faith in that which I cannot see.

I am having a crisis of faith in beliefs I once held as true.

Going To Beneficial Mindsets Like >>

Having faith in the unseen and a bigger plan

Being intrigued by the mysteries of the universe

Being an independent thinker and truth-seeker

Being curious about universal patterns and cycles

Understanding the fleeting nature of reality

Being in communion with your surroundings

Honoring the role of others in your life

Looking beyond yourself and your immediate surroundings

Showing up in beneficial mindsets like:

I embrace the interconnectedness of all parts in the grander plan.

I feel a profound sense of belonging and harmony within the universe.

I trust in the unseen forces that shape my existence and purpose, and I know I play a role in all decisions.

I am experiencing a transformation of faith, opening myself to new beliefs and understanding.

TRANSLATING YOUR PET'S BEHAVIOR

In moments of crisis with our pets, whether due to illness, transition, or being lost, it's vital to embrace faith in the grander scheme of life. Our pet's journeys are intertwined with ours, and their experiences are lessons for both of us. As you face these challenges and let go of judgment and attachment to outcomes, these situations become opportunities for growth, understanding, and profound new connections with our animal companions.

What new abilities or insights are emerging as a response to this crisis?

What possibilities open up if you look at the bigger picture?

What other relationships or experiences in your life have transcended the physical?

What does this current crisis illuminate about past grief or difficult situations?

Where else in your life could you have more faith?

What new abilities or insights are emerging as a response to this crisis?

Moments of crisis with our pets become an opportunity to awaken deep questions we may not have dealt with before that give more insight into our abilities, beliefs, and self. They encourage us to lean into existing or new abilities and philosophies. When a health crisis occurs with your animal companion, it can act as a catalyst to help you open up to new paths and opportunities. With a sick pet, you might discover new interests, from healthier diets to spiritual practices like transcendental meditation or yoga. These interests may have been lingering in the background but gain importance when they become viable solutions to manage behavioral or physical symptoms.

A lost pet may be serving a purpose beyond their physical presence in our life. They also may be an opportunity to develop new abilities and perspectives, such as honing your intuition, learning about map-dowsing skills, or learning to sense your pet's energy in different ways. Through their wisdom, our pets guide us toward a deeper understanding of energy, preparing us for a more profound connection with the world around us.

Practical Insight: Explore journaling, art, or talking to a counselor to express your feelings and memories. Use this time to focus on self-care, allowing yourself to heal and find the insights that come with the process. Lean into new modalities and abilities, such as hands-on healing and animal communication.

What possibilities open up if you look at the bigger picture?
When we look at the bigger picture, the loss of a pet can help us appreciate the significance of our connection and its infinite nature. We learn that love transcends physical boundaries and the bond we share with our pet continues beyond the physical plane. Our pet's legacy may inspire us to make a positive impact on other animals or engage in activities that promote the well-being of pets everywhere. In some cases, given their lifespan, the loss of a pet can be the first insight into death and questioning what happens later. For kids, the loss of a pet fish may bring this subject to light, and for an adult, the death of a furry companion can even prepare us for the loss of a parent.

Practical Insight: Embrace the idea that your pet's energy and love live on. Channel your emotions into creating positive change, such as volunteering at animal shelters, supporting animal rescue organizations, or even starting a project that honors your pet's memory. In doing so, you can find a sense of purpose and connection beyond the physical realm.

What other relationships or experiences in your life have transcended the physical?

The loss of a pet can be a profound reminder of the transcendent nature of relationships and experiences. The emotional and energetic connection we share with our pets transcends the physical world, and their presence can be felt in memories and the ongoing love they offer. For our pets, the transition is not the end but rather the beginning of a new way to collaborate, one that is more limitless and in a different form. They continue to be our partners, guiding us from a place beyond the physical world. It is not uncommon to sense their presence on the bed or hear their pet tag jingle even after they've crossed over. These experiences can open your heart to other connections that extend beyond the here and now.

Practical Insight: Reflect on the relationships and experiences in your life that transcend the physical, like a grandmother who passed away, a childhood friend you lost touch with, or even a career you've retired from. Consider the impact of these connections on your personal growth and well-being. By acknowledging and nurturing these transcendent relationships and experiences, you can find comfort and strength in times of loss and crisis.

What does this current crisis illuminate about past grief or difficult situations?

Losing a beloved pet, especially one that has transitioned, can lead to newfound abilities and insights. Grief often opens the door to a deeper understanding of the bond between humans and their animal companions. It teaches us to process complex emotions and develop resilience, creating opportunities to strengthen our emotional intelligence and gain insight into the beauty of shared experiences. Past grief or moments of crisis have likely helped you understand the depths of human emotions and the importance of compassion and empathy. The experience of losing a pet can deepen your capacity to connect with others who are also grieving. It offers insight into the shared human experience of loss. Current moments of crisis may serve to better understand past experiences. And in turn, that insight can help you through current challenges.

Practical Insight: Reach out to those who may be grieving the loss of a pet and offer a listening ear, empathy, and understanding. By sharing your own journey, you can provide solace and guidance to those in need.

Where else in your life could you have more faith?
Experiencing doubt is a natural response to the loss or illness of a pet and an important part of the grieving process. Doubt may arise in the form of questioning your decisions, second-guessing your actions, or doubting the fairness of the situation. By acknowledging doubt, you can gain insight into your emotions and work through these feelings until you are able to create room for faith. Losing a pet can challenge your faith in the goodness of life and the universe. Yet, it also presents an opportunity to cultivate faith in the healing power of time, the resilience of the human spirit, and the enduring nature of relationships. It reminds you that moments of crisis can lead to renewal and growth.

Practical Insight: As you navigate the healing process, focus on cultivating faith in coping with loss and adversity. If it creeps in, use doubt as a catalyst for introspection and personal growth and a means to help you find clarity and acceptance. Seek solace in rituals, practices, or belief systems that resonate with your spiritual journey. By doing so, you can find comfort and strength in moments of crisis, knowing that you are part of a larger, supportive universe.

PRACTICAL CONSIDERATIONS

Pet parenting can bring us so much joy, but when our animal companions are sick, have transitioned, or have gone missing, we may experience a crisis of faith. With little other choice, this forces us to take a step back and trust in the big picture.

Sometimes, "bad" or even devastating things happen to our pets, and we do not fully understand why. Although many of us believe things happen according to a bigger plan, it can be difficult to understand and accept that when we can't see the blueprint laid out in front of us.

That's when we are asked to do what sometimes feels like the impossible: have faith that everything is unfolding as it should, without judgment or attachment to the outcome.

We are being asked to trust that every situation, pleasant or not, holds wisdom and opportunity for growth.

Health Crisis/Sick Pets

When dealing with the physical issues in our pets, we have the benefit of having them alongside us, providing real-time clues and feedback on what to look for next. Tools like the Translating Beyond Behavior℠ roadmap provide a quick reference and a starting point for understanding what specific physical conditions mirror energetically.

But while external resources are valuable, it's also crucial to turn to your inner wisdom. As you explore courses of treatment, feel into what you're most drawn to and why. Notice any judgments or fears around treatment methods and where those beliefs originate.

Consider where in your body you feel decisions about your pet's well-being. Is it in your mind or your gut? Are you muscle-testing on your pet's behalf?

Examine your attachments, especially in terms of the healing timeframe. If the condition is severe, consider the possibility of your pet transitioning. Address any judgments or fears you might hold around that outcome. Gain a better understanding of any preconceptions, and trust yourself more when swift action is required.

If your animal companion is in good health, you can look back at past physical issues and explore whether there are any energetic parallels with the benefit of hindsight.

When caring for sick pets

Be Attentive. Pay close attention to your pet's needs and any changes in their behavior. Your keen observation is essential in providing the care they require.

Seek Veterinary Care. Seek professional veterinary care promptly. Consult with experts who can diagnose and provide guidance on the best course of action for your pet's specific condition.

Offer Emotional Support. Spend quality time with your sick pet, offering comfort, reassurance, and love. Your emotional support can make a significant difference in their well-being.

Offer Energetic Support. In addition to traditional forms of treatment, hands-on energetic modalities like reiki, visualizations, space clearings, or even leveraging healing crystals around the home can increase your pet's well-being and assist in their recovery.

Create a Calm Environment. Ensure their environment is calm and peaceful, as a serene atmosphere can aid their recovery. Minimize stressors and provide a safe, comforting space for them.

Engage in Gentle Activities. Engage in gentle activities your pet enjoys, such as soothing massages, snuffle mats, or quiet play sessions.

These activities can provide comfort and help your pet feel loved and cherished during their recovery.

Transitioned Pets

Coping with the transition of a beloved pet is a profound and often heart-wrenching experience. Yet, it can also be a time of deep reflection and understanding, offering insights into the unique and beautiful way our animal companions perceive this transition.

Here are some insights on the process shared across various animal communication sessions:

Acclimation through Solitude. As pets near the end of their lives, they may seek solitude, spending more time alone in different spaces. This behavior, akin to a game of Hide & Seek, helps both pet and human acclimate to the inevitable separation when they have left their physical bodies. It's a gentle preparation, a way for pets to gradually disconnect from the physical world and the human to be attuned to their energetic and telepathic connection that will allow their relationship and communication to endure even once disembodied.

Dealing with Pain. To our animal companions, the body is merely a means to an end. This allows them to be free from pain or suffering, sidestepping their physical selves as needed and returning to them once the pain or discomfort has subsided. They do not need to experience pain or be in agony as humans often do during physical distress.

Final Moments of Embodiment. The final moments with your pet can be particularly poignant. Many pet parents focus on these moments, considering whether they were present, advocated appropriately, or spent enough time together leading up to their transition. It's natural to reflect on these moments and wonder if everything was done right. However, it's essential to remember that in their wisdom, our pets focus on the entirety of the relationship and time spent together. They do not fixate on their final days or moments, as we often do. Their perspective encompasses all the shared experiences, the love, and the bond forged throughout their lives.

Embracing Disembodying. Just as we feel the release of stress and pressures when we come home and shed our work clothes, our animal companions perceive disembodying as a simple and liberating process. They effortlessly step out of their physical bodies without emotional attachments to it, lacking the same connection to their physical form that humans often possess. It's a natural and almost joyous release, a return to a state of pure energy and freedom. When pets transition—whether peacefully or suddenly—they simply step out of their physical bodies. It's a peaceful release from the confines of the physical world, a transition that brings them comfort.

Unwavering Connection. Unlike humans, our pets don't require a physical form to feel a strong, unwavering connection to us. As you process your grief and guilt, you'll likely sense your beloved companion still near you. Their constant companionship persists, much as it did when they were in their physical form. It's a reminder that love transcends the physical, and their presence remains a source of comfort and reassurance.

Honoring a Transitioned Pet

Allow yourself to grieve and seek support from friends, family, or pet loss support groups. It's essential to acknowledge and process your emotions during this challenging time; seeking support can provide a sense of understanding and connection. This also holds true for other pets in the pack who may be grieving or adjusting to the changes in the pack.

Create Memorials. Cherish the special moments you shared by creating a memorial or keepsake in your pet's memory. These physical reminders serve as a beautiful tribute to the love and companionship you experienced together.

Channel Grief Positively. Consider volunteering at or supporting an animal charity in your pet's name, turning your grief into a positive force. This allows you to honor your pet's memory by making a meaningful difference in the lives of other animals in need.

Practice Self-Care. Focus on self-care as you navigate the emotional toll of losing a pet. Engage in activities that bring you joy and comfort. Remember that it's okay to mourn the loss, but it's also important to celebrate the happiness your pet brought to your life. Self-care helps you heal, be compassionate with yourself, and find solace during this emotional journey.

Lost Pets

Navigating the distressing situation of a lost pet can be emotionally challenging for any pet parent. When faced with a lost pet, the mind runs wild. We are called upon to transcend the constructs of the mind and have faith and trust in the bigger picture in uncertain circumstances while practicing non-judgment and non-attachment to outcomes. These are some practical and mindful steps you can take.

Conduct a Thorough Search. Begin by conducting a thorough search in your neighborhood. Cover as much ground as possible, and be mindful of places where your pet might seek refuge.

Alert Local Resources. Contact local animal shelters and use community platforms to spread the word about your lost pet. The more people who are aware, the higher the chances of reuniting with your furry friend.

Embrace Calm and Hope. Stay calm, present, and hopeful while searching, as pets can often sense scattered energy, which adds to any confusion they may be experiencing. Your presence of mind and stable energy can serve as a beacon to guide them home.

Secure Your Home. Ensure your home is a safe and secure environment for your pet in case they return on their own. Leave food, water, and familiar items outside your home so they are reassured that they've arrived at the right place.

Community Support. Reach out to your community for help, as their support can be invaluable during these times. Neighbors and friends can assist in the search effort.

Golden Thread Exercise. Visualize a golden thread leading from your heart to your pet's heart. Allow this to be a pathway for energetic connection, telepathic communication, and a beacon leading your pet back to you.

Keep the Faith. Maintain your faith that many lost pets find their way back home. Your patience and positive energy can be a guiding light to lead them back to safety.

Additional Considerations

Pets Preparing Us for Bigger Loss. The death of a beloved pet can prepare us for the inevitable passing of other loved ones in our lives. This experience is especially impactful when our animal companion is the first time we face losing a cherished member of the pack. For children whose beloved furry dog passes, it provides an opportunity to explore grief and the concepts of death, transcendence, and an afterlife. As adults, the loss of a pet may serve as a gentle preparation for the eventual care and passing of elderly parents or other close family members. Through these experiences, our pets not only enrich our lives with companionship but also become poignant guides, imparting valuable insights into the cycle of life, loss, and the enduring nature of love and connection.

The Role of the Body. One consistent message I've received from pets during animal communication sessions is that they don't get hung up in the mindset of the disease. They are not as attached to their bodies as we are. The body is the vessel, but they mostly care about its role in allowing them to explore the world through their senses. When they feel good, they don't worry about whether that will change later in the day. If they don't feel well, they rest. They don't judge how they are feeling or extrapolate what that will mean for tomorrow and the next day. They stay in the experience and react to what their body tells them they need without lamenting or comparing it to how they felt yesterday or will feel tomorrow.

CASE STUDIES

Case Study #1

Learning to Trust the Moments

In pet parenting, there comes a moment when we're faced with profound decisions about our furry companions, especially when they embark on the journey of transitioning from this life. It's a sacred and deeply personal crossroads that each pet parent must navigate in their own unique way. Such was the case with Toby, a gentle and wise chihuahua who had become an integral part of his human's life.

As Toby's time in this world approached its twilight, his pet parent was inundated with a whirlwind of emotions, grappling with whether to intervene in her beloved companion's transition process or allow nature to run its course. It was an emotional rollercoaster marked by uncertainty and the weight of the unknown.

When considering the prospect of helping Toby transition, her mind swirled with predictions and worries about what the next weeks might bring him in terms of pain and discomfort. She was trying to make an impossible decision based on uncertainty and fear about what the future might hold. But Toby's situation seemed to change from hour to hour. Although Toby may have been struggling in the morning, mid-afternoon he seemed comfortable.

In this delicate moment, the pet parent tuned into her intuitive connection with Toby and was guided to adhere to a simple yet profound principle: any decision on whether to intervene would be through the lens of "*Is this the right moment?*" Instead of making her decision about whether to help Toby transition based on the perceived quality of life—or lack thereof—of his remaining days, the pet parent was directed to trust her instincts, one moment at a time. It was an invitation to make decisions for the here and now, a shift from future forecasting that often led to doubt and indecision.

Toby's pet mom began to make decisions, focusing on providing the utmost care and love in one brief span of time. In the morning, she'd ask herself to decide whether it was the right moment to intervene in Toby's transition "just for this morning."

As the afternoon sun painted the room in warm hues, she once again revisited the decision grounded in "just for this afternoon." And when evening arrived, they continued to honor Toby's journey by asking what was the best decision just for that evening.

In this practice of moment-to-moment presence, something remarkable happened. The uncertainty of the future and the impact of the pet parent's decisions based on future casting gradually gave way to a profound sense of clarity. Each choice, small yet significant, was guided by an intuition based on how Toby seemed in that moment. And with those parameters, her decisions were made confidently and effortlessly.

As she cherished the remaining time with Toby—which ultimately spanned weeks longer than any vet would have predicted—his pet parent realized that these smaller, heartfelt decisions focused on shorter periods of time not only built trust in the bigger picture and faith that she understood what was needed in each moment but provided her and Toby peace and time to focus on creating loving experiences they both would relish.

Practical Insight: Toby's journey teaches us the power of embracing the present moment, especially when faced with significant decisions regarding our pet's health. By trusting our instincts and focusing on making choices for this moment, we can find clarity, strength, and a deeper connection with our pets and ourselves during times of transition and uncertainty.

Case Study #2

Our Animal Companions' Multifaceted Missions

Just as people and opportunities enter our lives to be part of a greater purpose, our pets have their roles and purposes to fulfill. One case study illustrates the power of our pets' missions, which can sometimes extend beyond the life we share as a pack. This journey revealed a pup's deeper purpose: to uncover and rescue other pets in dire conditions.

Two pet siblings went missing, setting the stage for a collaborative effort to energetically track and guide them home. As the harrowing search unfolded over days, only one of the dogs managed to return safely.

But the story did not end there. The missing sister revealed specific coordinates and landmarks leading to what would be her final resting place in a field. When setting out to find her, the pet parent discovered a rudimentary puppy mill in that location. These findings were reported to the authorities, resulting in the rescue of numerous other furry friends suffering in dire conditions.

In hindsight, the bigger picture emerges surrounding these two pets. The dog who did not return home fulfilled a heroic role, which her pet parents could never have predicted at the beginning of this ordeal. Her legacy became one of compassion and rescue, touching the lives of countless other animals in need. Although it is heartbreaking that both pups did not return home safely, this dog's special story serves as a testament to our animal companions' profound and often mysterious missions that transcend our immediate understanding and can impact the lives of others in ways we might not have considered.

Practical Insight: This case study encourages us to broaden our perspective on the roles of our animal companions. It highlights that our pets might have missions and purposes that extend beyond their immediate relationships with us. The story showcases the incredible potential for pets to impact the lives of others and serve heroic roles, even when the outcomes are not what we anticipated.

Activities

MINDFULLY RECONNECTING

As we embark on this guided meditation, we will explore a sacred journey to connect with our beloved pets and departed loved ones, embracing the enduring bonds that transcend our physical realm. Find a tranquil space free from distraction. In this stillness, allow the words to guide you deeply and lovingly, knowing you can return to this meditation anytime you'd like to reconnect with a beloved companion who has transitioned.

Let's get started by finding a comfortable position, seated or lying down. Place your hands on your lap, over your heart, or by your sides. Your pet may join you physically or come on the journey energetically. You may find that your current pet joins you, or perhaps a pet that is no longer with you will come along, as our animal companions never truly leave our side.

Just take the next few moments to settle into the journey, wherever you are.

Now, when you're ready, close your eyes and bring your attention to your breath. Breathe in deeply through your nose, and let it out through your mouth with sound. Continue taking those slow, deep breaths. And with each breath, remember that you are connected to all things and that all things are connected to you.

Allow yourself to simply follow the natural rhythm of your breath….and join me and your animal companion on a beautiful journey connecting back to loved ones, experiences, or memories from your past.

Picture yourself seated in the place where you feel most at peace and most connected. It may be in a field, in a forest, on a beach, or in a lovely meditation room. It may be somewhere you remember from childhood, a place you frequent often, or a space you have created in your mind's eye.

Take a breath and connect deeply with your own body. Appreciate how your unique energetic essence permeates your being, beginning at your feet, filling up your shins, thighs, hips, and every single cell, fiber, and muscle of your body. Watch how your own essential energy spills out into your aura and how your aura interplays with the energy surrounding you. You feel relaxed, connected, and expansive.

Now call in an energy you would like to connect with that has disembodied, transitioned, or is prominently in your past. It may be a pet that has crossed over, a loved one who is no longer with you, a guide you'd like to contact, or simply a remembrance or experience from a long time ago.

Hold that intention in your heart as you close your mind's eye. Focus on the rhythm of your breath until you feel a gentle gust of wind blow by you. Open your mind's eye to see that the energy you called in to reconnect with has arrived and is now seated next to you at your right-hand side.

You delight and feel a lovely warmth wash over you at the comfort of being reunited in this way.

Take a moment to connect with that energy, whether basking in its vibration, sharing how much you love them, asking any questions you may have, or simply sharing anything you felt was left unsaid.

Take a moment to listen to the response.

With your dear companion's energy still to the right of you, allow them to show you people, animals, experiences, or opportunities that will be entering your life. Observe these taking form just to your left, and understanding, excitement, and curiosity dawn upon you as you regard what the future holds for you.

Take a moment to anchor into the energy of what is to come, allowing your heart to prepare for and welcome those vibrations.

Next, you receive instruction to look just ahead of you. These are the people, energies, animals, dynamics, or situations that need your attention right now, in this current moment of your life.

Observe as they come into clarity just ahead of you. As you recognize and acknowledge each energy, experience, or person appearing before you, you feel a calm confidence that the key to assisting, shifting, and transforming them lies within you. You know what needs to be done in your heart, mind, and gut.

With that, you look back to your companion at your right-hand side. You share a loving moment together, thanking them for still being so present, involved, and supportive in your life.

They offer a loving gesture—one unique to them, for old time's sake—reminding you that your time together has not ended; it has simply changed and evolved.

They remind you that they remain a part of your energetic essence for all time, as you are lovingly and inextricably linked at a soul level.

You watch as what appears to be a golden dragonfly flies around your companion and, through the energy of their heart, weaves a trail of light in its wake. The golden dragonfly then links their heart with yours. It then does the same with all that joined you in this meditation—whether from the past, present, or future.

With that, the energy and consciousness of all who love and support you and your transformation across timelines and dimensions are linked, palpable, and always accessible to you as precious members of your soul pack.

Thank your companion for joining you on such a beautiful journey, and notice what you see, feel, sense, and hear as you return to your present state and surroundings.

Stay here for a few more moments, breathing in and out.

When you feel ready, gently open your eyes and wiggle your toes, returning to your body.
Take a moment to return to your surroundings, becoming more aware of the sounds around you.

Now, your journey is complete. Take a moment to jot down any sensations, impressions, or insights.

Feel free to revisit this meditation anytime you want to mindfully reconnect with animal companions, people, memories, or experiences from your past.

Scan this QR code to access this guided meditation as a downloadable MP3.

In Summation
NahMuttStay®

What a journey we have been on, exploring your pet's behaviors, gathering energetic clues from them, and applying the insights to our lives.

Beyond being a play on words, *'NahMuttStay'* carries a profound message that reminds us to embrace the profound connection that exists between us and our pets. While the term 'Namaste' signifies recognizing the divine light humans share, our pets invite us into a similar sacred space with them. Their actions and behaviors reveal the same subtle yet transformative message – *'The divine light in me bows to the divine light in you.'* In essence, they propose and initiate a unique connection that invites us to recognize the magic deeper within ourselves.

If you take away anything, I hope it is the understanding that some of the most powerful teachers in our lives are the ones closest to us. For many of us, that is our dog, cat, horse, guinea pig, or bird. And their behavior is one of the ways our animals teach and communicate with us. When we learn to interpret our pet's signals and efficiently translate our pet's behavior, we create meaningful and long-lasting transformations for ourselves and our furry friends.

I hope you'll leverage this book to more effectively translate your pet's behavior and that it helps you realize that you are already communicating with your pet in profound and transformative ways.

Here are some highlights of the lessons our animal companions shared with us.

Everything Has Meaning

Our pets teach us to see beyond immediate appearances and observe and experience our surroundings and relationships more deeply. Everything we encounter throughout our day can point us toward growth and new understandings. As we interpret those signs and piece them together, a bigger picture formed by our attitudes, actions, and motivations reveals itself. Once we step into a broader perspective, our relationships with our animal companions become richer, fuller, and more transformative.

You Have the Power to Create Change

Our pets are here to help us change old stories and limiting mindsets. When we acknowledge that our behavior affects outcomes in our lives, then we trust that shifts in our behavior can alter how situations and relationships ultimately play out. We are not merely spectators. We are in control of how we choose to interpret our pets' behaviors—whether naughty or nice—and from there, we can choose how to proceed. When we opt for new paths, we create a more intentional future alongside our animal companions.

Boundaries Are Essential

Setting healthy boundaries preserves our physical, emotional, and energetic integrity and the full expression of ourselves. If we avoid doing this, we become disconnected from our needs, desires, and creativity, falling into patterns of senseless sacrifice and martyrdom. Many of us suppress our needs for fear of being selfish or feeling that our needs don't matter. When our pets ask us to give them loving boundaries, what they are really doing is drawing attention to our need to do the same in other areas of our lives as well.

Home Is Where the Heart Is

Make yourself at home in the present. Our pets teach us that to be open-hearted, we must live in the moment, avoiding beating ourselves up over coulda, shoulda, wouldas of the past, or the "what ifs" of the future. They show us how to be in gratitude and accept, appreciate, and nurture what we currently have. Our pets are experts at teaching compassion, showing us the companionship and respect we all deserve, and how to love who we are today and what we presently contribute to the world.

Get Your Bark On

Our pets help us identify and speak our truth, ultimately helping us find our authentic voice. They inspire us to speak up for ourselves and on behalf of those who cannot do so, like the animals. Our voice instills into the zeitgeist that their needs and rights are just as important as those of any other sentient being. We can speak of compassion, awareness, and our interconnectedness, and avoid using terms like "pet owner" opting for "pet guardian" instead. Our pets remind us that when we uncover and speak our truth in every area of our lives, we radiate authenticity, feel more fulfilled, and inspire others to do the same.

But Most of All

Our pets want us to see ourselves through their eyes as the wonderful, multidimensional, unique, and beautiful souls we are. They are honored to be learning alongside us, just as I am honored to acknowledge their contributions alongside you, co-creating this new path forward in pet guardianship.

Happy journeying on this path of self-discovery with your animal companion.

Nah Mutt Stay!

Bonus Materials

In addition to the practical and energetic content presented in each chapter of this book, we've curated bonus materials to further enrich your learning experience. These supplementary resources are designed to deepen your understanding and provide additional tools for implementing the teachings discussed. We trust that you'll find value and enjoyment in exploring these bonus materials as you embark on your journey of transformation and growth.

Scan this QR code to access the bonus materials.

About the Author

Denise Mange is a certified dog trainer, animal communicator, pet numerologist, and founder of Pet Prana®. She believes that everyday interactions with our pets have the power to transform us.

After a decade of working at some of the most prestigious advertising agencies in New York City, Denise left Madison Avenue to work with pets and their humans. Her mindful approach to pet training combines traditional training with numerology, meditation, and energetic considerations of pet guardianship to foster true collaboration, heart-centered connections, and a deeper understanding of the lessons your animal companions are here to share.

As a thought leader in her field, Denise's articles have been featured in publications spanning from pet guardianship to conscious living, and she has appeared on numerous radio shows and podcasts. Denise has sat on expert panels, been a featured speaker on keynote stages, and helped develop the pet category for a top-rated wellness app.

Dig Into Online Courses

Through Pet Prana®, Denise offers best-in-show pet training classes, one-of-a-kind courses on energetic aspects of pet guardianship, remote animal communication sessions, and free resources to help you go deeper with the animal companions in your life.

Unlike any other pet resource available, fetch our rare breed online pet courses combining traditional training with energetic considerations of pet guardianship at www.petprana.com.

A Mindful Approach to Pet Training

Enjoy these on-demand instructional and training tutorials on the most important topics in raising a puppy or getting a long-time companion back on track.

Energetic Connection with Pets

Go beyond behavior, whether learning to mindfully translate your pet's actions through chakra work or opening up to your intuition through pets.

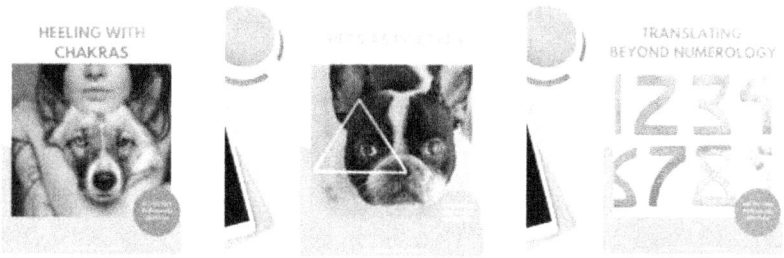

Scan this QR code to access the course descriptions, or find them at petprana.com.

Notes

Printed in Great Britain
by Amazon